THE CANADIAN BAR ASSOCIATION

CODE OF PROFESSIONAL CONDUCT

ADOPTED BY COUNCIL, AUGUST 1987

CODE OF PROFESSIONAL CONDUCT

ISBN 0-920742-28-9

Published by The Canadian Bar Association

The Association gratefully acknowledges the generous support granted by
Carswell Legal Publications and the Canadian Bar Insurance Association.

The Special Committee

Robert P. Fraser, Q.C., Chairman
Mark M. Orkin, Q.C., Committee Counsel
The Honourable George S. Finlayson
The Honourable George S. Cumming
Barbara Stanley
G.R. Schmitt, Q.C.
Donald S. McKercher, Q.C.
Knox B. Foster, Q.C.
Edward L. Greenspan, Q.C.
J.J. Carthy, Q.C.
M. le bâtonnier Guy Pépin, Q.C.
J. William E. Mingo, Q.C.

Technical Staff:

George Boros, Director of Resource and Professional Development
Stephen Hanson, Senior Director of Communications
Kathryn J. Randle, Editor

First Printing 1974
Revised and adopted by Council, August 1987

© Canadian Bar Association 1988
   Suite 902, 50 O'Connor
   Ottawa, Ontario
   K1P 6L2

CONTENTS

Page

Foreword v

Preface vii

Interpretation xi

Chapter I — Integrity 1

Chapter II — Competence and Quality of Service 5

Chapter III — Advising Clients 9

Chapter IV — Confidential Information 13

Chapter V — Impartiality and Conflict of Interest between Clients 17

Chapter VI — Conflict of Interest between Lawyer and Client 23

Chapter VII — Outside Interests and the Practice of Law 27

Chapter VIII — Preservation of Clients' Property 31

Chapter IX — The Lawyer as Advocate 35

Chapter X — The Lawyer in Public Office 45

Chapter XI — Fees 49

Chapter XII — Withdrawal 53

Chapter XIII — The Lawyer and the Administration of Justice 59

Chapter XIV — Advertising, Solicitation and Making Legal Services Available 63

Chapter XV — Responsibility to the Profession Generally 67

Chapter XVI — Responsibility to Lawyers Individually 69

Chapter XVII — Practice by Unauthorized Persons 73

Chapter XVIII — Public Appearances and Public Statements by Lawyers 77

Chapter XIX — Avoiding Questionable Conduct 81

Abbreviations 85

Bibliography 87

Index 89

The Canadian
Bar Association
acknowledges the
valuable contribution
of **The Canadian
Bar Insurance Association**
towards the
publication of The Code
of Professional Conduct.

L'Association du
Barreau canadien remercie
**l'Association d'assurances
du Barreau canadien** pour
sa généreuse contribution
permettant la publication
du Code de déontologie
professionnelle.

FOREWORD

At the meeting of the National Executive Committee of The Canadian Bar Association in January of 1984, a resolution was adoted unanimously to review the 1974 Code of Professional Conduct. The then President Robert McKercher, Q.C. appointed Robert P. Fraser, Q.C. to chair the Committee to Revise The Code of Professional Conduct.

The National Council of the Canadian Bar Association in August of 1987 adopted without a dissenting vote the Revised Code of Professional Conduct (1987).

In his report to Council, Robert P. Fraser, Q.C. stated:

"You will recall that this Association approved a Code in 1974. Since that time, that Code has been used by and large, as the authority in terms of ethics and discipline matters by all Law Societies in Canada, and to a lesser extent, by the Barreau du Québec. It has been adopted by some provinces in its entirety, others have used it as the basis of their own provincial publication."

In drafting the new Code, the Committee began its work with the conscious decision to build upon the 1974 document, (delivered to The Canadian Bar Association by the then Committee Chairman S.E. Fennell, Q.C., Past President of the CBA), and to bring forward only those changes that reflect the realities of practising law in today's society.

In adopting the 1987 Code of Professional Conduct, The Canadian Bar Association recognized the extraordinary effort on the part of the Committee in bringing to realization the revised document after numerous consultations with Council, CBA Branches, and the Law Societies. The Association is grateful to the Committee for its professional contribution to the practice of law in Canada.

The Honourable Jean Bazin, Q.C.
President
Ottawa, June 1988

PREFACE[1]

The legal profession has developed over the centuries to meet a public need for legal services on a professional basis. Traditionally, this has involved the provision of advice and representation to protect or advance the rights, liberties and property of a client by a trusted adviser with whom the client has a personal relationship and whose integrity, competence and loyalty are assured.[2]

In order to satisfy this need for legal services adequately, lawyers and the quality of service they provide must command the confidence and respect of the public. This can only be achieved if lawyers establish and maintain a reputation for both integrity and high standards of legal skill and care. The lawyers of many countries in the world, despite differences in their legal systems, practices, procedures and customs, have all imposed upon themselves substantially the same basic standards. Those standards invariably place their main emphasis on integrity and competence.

In Canada, the provincial legislatures have entrusted to the legal profession through its governing bodies responsibility for maintaining standards of professional conduct and for disciplining lawyers who fail to meet them. Generally, the preparation and publication of codes of ethics and professional conduct have been left to the profession. It is a responsibility that must be accepted and carried out by the profession as a whole.

The pertinent laws in Canada use various terms to describe conduct that subjects the lawyer to discipline, for example, "professional misconduct", "conduct unbecoming" and "acts derogatory to the honour or dignity of the Bar". Some statutes also provide that disciplinary action may be taken if a lawyer is convicted of an indictable offence, or for "misappropriation or wrongful conversion", or "gross negligence" or for conduct "incompatible with the best interests of the public or the members of the [Law] Society", or for breach of the applicable statute itself or the rules made under it.[3]

With few exceptions the statutes do not specify the kinds of conduct that will subject a lawyer to discipline. For its part, the Code does not attempt to define professional misconduct or conduct unbecoming, nor does it try to evaluate the relative importance of the various rules or the gravity of a breach of any of them. Those functions are the responsibility of the various governing bodies. The rules that follow are therefore intended to serve as a guide, and the commentaries and notes appended to them are illustrative only. By enunciating principles of what is and is not acceptable professional conduct, the Code is designed to assist governing bodies and practitioners alike in determining whether in a given case the conduct is acceptable, thus furthering the process of self-government.

The essence of professional responsibility is that the lawyer must act at all times *uberrimae fidei*, with utmost good faith to the court, to the client, to other lawyers, and to members of the public. Given the many and varied demands to which the lawyer is subject, it is inevitable that problems will arise. No set of rules can foresee every possible situation, but the ethical principles set out in the Code are intended to provide a framework within which the lawyer may, with courage and dignity, provide the high quality of legal services that a complex and ever-changing society demands.[4]

The extent to which each lawyer's conduct should rise above the minimum standards set by the Code is a matter of personal decision. The lawyer who would enjoy the respect and confidence of the community as well as of other members of the legal profession must strive to maintain the highest possible degree of ethical conduct. The greatness and strength of the legal profession depend on high standards of professional conduct that permit no compromise.

The Code of Professional Conduct that follows is to be understood and applied in the light of its primary concern for the protection of the public interest. This principle is implicit in the legislative grants of self-government referred to above. Inevitably, the practical application of the Code to the diverse situations that confront an active profession in a changing society will reveal gaps, ambiguities and apparent inconsistencies.[5] In such cases, the principle of protection of the public interest will serve to guide the practitioner to the applicable principles of ethical conduct and the true intent of the Code.

NOTES

1. The footnotes relate the provisions of the Code to pertinent earlier Codes, rulings, by-laws, statutes, judicial dicta, text books and articles, as well as to certain other materials. They are selective, not exhaustive, and merely supplement the text. For abbreviations and bibliography, see pages 85 and 87.

2. "The core of the proposition is that problems of . . . rights or property call for a personal relationship with a trusted adviser, whose discretion is absolute, who serves no master but his client, and whose competence is assured. The codes and traditions of the professions who supply these services support the basic proposition. They also display the uniformity that its truth would lead one to expect." *Bennion*, p. 16.

3. Abstract of disciplinary provisions:
    Alberta: *Legal Profession Act*, R.S.A. 1980, c. L-9
    s. 47 "conduct incompatible with the best interests of the public or the members of the Society"
    "tends to harm the standing of the legal profession generally"

    British Columbia: *Barristers and Solicitors Act*, R.S.B.C. 1979, c. 26
    s. 50 "misappropriation or wrongful conversion"
    "professional misconduct"
    "conduct unbecoming a member"
    "breach of this Act or the rules made under it"
    s. 55 "convicted of an indictable offence"

    Manitoba: *Law Society Act*, R.S.M. 1970, c. L-100
    s. 45 "professional misconduct"

"conduct unbecoming a barrister, solicitor, or student"

New Brunswick: *Barristers Society Act*, 1931, S.N.B., c. 50 as am. by S.N.B. 1954, c. 99

s. 19 "professional misconduct"
default *re* clients' moneys
breach of Act or regulation

Newfoundland: *Law Society Act*, R.S.N. 1970, c. 201

s. 37 "conduct unbecoming a barrister, solicitor, student-at-law or articled clerk"

Nova Scotia: *Barristers and Solicitors Act*, R.S.N.S. c. B-2

s. 29 "professional misconduct"
"conduct unbecoming a barrister or articled clerk"
s. 31 "absconding, insane or insolvent"

Ontario: *Law Society Act*, R.S.O. 1980, c. 233

s. 34 "professional misconduct"
"conduct unbecoming a barrister and solicitor"
s. 38 "conduct unbecoming a student member"

Prince Edward Island: *Law Society and Legal Profession Act*, R.S.P.E.I. 1974, c. L-9

s. 27 "professional misconduct"
"conduct unbecoming a member"

Quebec: *Bar Act*, R.S.Q. 1977, c. B-1

s. 107 "derogatory to the honour or dignity of the Bar or prejudicial to the discipline of its members"
"position or office . . . incompatible with the practice of the profession of advocate"
"occupation, industry or trade carried on or the position held is incompatible with the honour or dignity of the Bar"
s. 111 "conviction of an indictable offence"

Saskatchewan: *Legal Profession Act*, R.S.S. c. L-10

s. 59 "conduct unbecoming a barrister and solicitor"
s. 70 "convicted of an indictable offence"

England: *Cordery on Solicitors* (7th ed., 1981), p. 333
". . . because he has been guilty of an act or omission for which the Act or some other statute prescribes that penalty, or because he has committed an act of misconduct which renders him unfit to be permitted to continue in practice."
(at p. 335): "Misconduct which makes a solicitor unfit to continue in practice may be divided into three kinds: criminal conduct, professional misconduct and unprofessional conduct."
(at p. 336): "The jurisdiction is not limited to cases where the misconduct charged amounts to an indictable offence, or is professional in character, but extends to all cases where the solicitor's conduct is 'unprofessional', i.e., such as renders him unfit to be an officer of the court."

"Is it a personally disgraceful offence or is it not? Ought any respectable solicitor to be called upon to enter into that intimate discourse with (the offender) which is necessary between two solicitors even though they are acting for opposite parties?" per Lord Esher M.R., in *Re Weare* (1893), 2 Q.B. 439 at 446 (C.A.).

"Counsel . . . takes the position that the expressions (unprofessional conduct and professional misconduct) are synonymous . . . I agree . . . that the phrases are often used interchangeably but cannot agree that this is always so . . . . Accepting as I do that the terms are not synonymous . . .", per McKay J. in *Re Novak and Law Society* (1973) 31 D.L.R. (3d) 89 at 102 (B.C.S.C.).

4.   "The law and its institutions change as social conditions change. They must

change if they are to preserve, much less advance, the political and social values from which they derive their purposes and their life. This is true of the most important of legal institutions, the profession of law. The profession, too, must change when conditions change in order to preserve and advance the social values that are its reason for being." Cheatham, *Availability of Legal Services: The Responsibility of the Individual Lawyer and the Organized Bar* (1965) 12 U.C.L.A.L. Rev. 438, 440.

5.   "It is not possible to frame a set of rules which will particularize all the duties of the lawyer in all the varied relations of his professional life . . .". Sask. *Preamble.*

INTERPRETATION

In this Code the field of professional conduct and ethics is divided into nineteen chapters, each of which contains a short statement of a rule or principle followed by commentary and notes. Although this division gives rise to some overlapping of subjects, the principle of integrity enunciated in Chapter I underlies the entire Code so that some of the rules in subsequent chapters represent particular applications of the basic rule set out in Chapter I. Again there are instances where substantially the same comment appears more then once. Such duplication is considered desirable in order to provide clarity and emphasis and to reduce cross-references.

The commentary and notes to each rule contain a discussion of the ethical considerations involved, explanations, examples and other material designed to assist in the interpretation and understanding of the rule itself. Each rule should therefore be read with and interpreted in the light of the related commentary and notes.

Certain terms used in the Code require definition as follows:

"client"   means a person on whose behalf a lawyer renders or undertakes to render professional services;

"court"   includes conventional law courts and generally all judicial and quasi-judicial tribunals;

"Governing Body"   means the body charged under the laws of a particular jurisdiction with the duty of governing the legal profession (e.g., the Benchers, General Council, Convocation or Council);

"lawyer"   means an individual who is duly authorized to practise law;

"legal profession" refers to lawyers collectively;

"person"   includes a corporation or other legal entity, an association, partnership or other organization, the Crown in right of Canada or a province and the government of a state or any political subdivision thereof.

It will be noted that the term "lawyer" as defined above extends not only to those engaged in private practice but also to those who are employed on a full-time basis by governments, agencies, corporations and other organizations. An employer-employee relationship of this kind may give rise to special problems in the area of conflict of interest,[1] but in all matters involving integrity[2] and generally in all professional matters, if the requirements or demands of the employer conflict with the standards declared by the Code, the latter must govern.

NOTES

1. See Chap. V.
2. See Chap. I. The involvement of various lawyers in The Watergate Affair most graphically illustrates some of the hazards.

CHAPTER I

INTEGRITY

RULE

The lawyer must discharge with integrity all duties owed to clients, the court, other members of the profession and the public.[1]

Commentary

Guiding Principles

1.   Integrity is the fundamental quality of any person who seeks to practise as a member of the legal profession. If the client is in any doubt about the lawyer's trustworthiness the essential element in the lawyer-client relationship will be missing. If personal integrity is lacking the lawyer's usefulness to the client and reputation within the profession will be destroyed regardless of how competent the lawyer may be.[2]

2.   The principle of integrity is a key element of each rule of the Code.

Disciplinary Action

3.   Dishonourable or questionable conduct on the part of the lawyer in either private life or professional practice will reflect adversely upon the lawyer, the integrity of the legal profession and the administration of justice as a whole.[3] If the conduct, whether within or outside the professional sphere, is such that knowledge of it would be likely to impair the client's trust in the lawyer as a professional consultant, a governing body may be justified in taking disciplinary action.[4]

Non-professional Activities

4.   Generally speaking, however, a governing body will not be concerned with the purely private or extra-professional activities of a lawyer that do not bring into question the integrity of the legal profession or the lawyer's professional integrity or competence.

NOTES

1. Cf. CBA-COD 1. *O.E.D.*: "Integrity ... soundness of moral principle, esp. in relation to truth and fair dealing; uprightness, honesty, sincerity, candour."
    Cf. IBA. "Introductory". "The rules of professional conduct enforced in various countries ... uniformly place the main emphasis upon the essential need for integrity and, thereafter, upon the duties owed by a lawyer to his client, to the Court, to other members of the legal profession and to the public at large."

2. "Integrity, probity or uprightness is a prized quality in almost every sphere of life .... The best assurance the client can have ... is the basic integrity of the professional consultant .... Sir Thomas Lund says that ... his reputation is the greatest asset a solicitor can have .... A reputation for integrity is an indivisible whole; it can therefore be lost by actions having little or nothing to do with the profession .... Integrity has many aspects and may be displayed (or not) in a wide variety of situations ... the preservation of confidences, the display of impartiality, the taking of full responsibility are all aspects of integrity. So is the question of competence .... *Integrity is the fundamental quality, whose absence vitiates all others.*" *Bennion, passim,* pp. 108-12 (emphasis added).

3. Illustrations of conduct that may infringe the Rule (and often other provisions of this Code) include:
    (a) committing any personally disgraceful or morally reprehensible offence that reflects upon the lawyer's integrity (whereof a conviction by a competent court would be *prima facie* evidence);
    (b) committing, whether professionally or in the lawyer's personal capacity, any act of fraud or dishonesty, e.g., by knowingly making a false tax return or falsifying a document, even without fraudulent intent, and whether or not prosecuted therefor;
    (c) making untrue representations or concealing material facts from a client with dishonest or improper motives;
    (d) taking improper advantage of the youth, inexperience, lack of education or sophistication, ill health, or unbusinesslike habits of a client;
    (e) misappropriating or dealing dishonestly with the client's monies;
    (f) receiving monies from or on behalf of a client expressly for a specific purpose and failing, without the client's consent, to pay them over for that purpose;
    (g) knowingly assisting, enabling or permitting any person to act fraudulently, dishonestly or illegally toward the lawyer's client;
    (h) failing to be absolutely frank and candid in all dealings with the Court, fellow lawyers and other parties to proceedings, subject always to not betraying the client's cause, abandoning the client's legal rights or disclosing the client's confidences;
    (i) failing, when dealing with a person not legally represented, to disclose material facts, e.g., the existence of a mortgage on a property being sold, or supplying false information, whether the lawyer is professionally representing a client or is concerned personally;
    (j) failure to honour the lawyer's word when pledged even though, under technical rules, the absence of writing might afford a legal defence.
    Other examples are specifically dealt with in subsequent chapters.
    (The foregoing are drawn largely from IBA A-1 to A-24 and from disciplinary records. For illustrative cases in the same area see, e.g., 36 *Halsbury* (3d) pp. 222-26 and *Orkin*, pp. 204-14. In *Re Weare* (1893), 2 Q.B. 439 (C.A.) the striking off of a solicitor who had knowingly rented his premises for use as a brothel was upheld by the Court.)
    As to the distinction between "professional misconduct" and "unprofessional conduct" in disciplinary proceedings, see note 3 to the *Preface, supra.*

4. Cf. IBA, Chapter 2.
"The public looks for a hallmark bestowed by a trusted professional body, and evidenced by entry on a register or members' list." (p. 36). "Membership of a . . . professional body is generally treated as an indication of good character in itself . . .", *Bennion*, p. 111.

CHAPTER II

COMPETENCE AND QUALITY OF SERVICE

RULE

(a) The lawyer owes the client a duty to be competent to perform any legal services undertaken on the client's behalf.[1]

(b) The lawyer should serve the client in a conscientious, diligent and efficient manner so as to provide a quality of service at least equal to that which lawyers generally would expect of a competent lawyer in a like situation.[2]

Commentary

Knowledge and Skill

1. Competence in the context of the first branch of this Rule goes beyond formal qualification to practise law. It has to do with the sufficiency of the lawyer's qualifications to deal with the matter in question. It includes knowledge, skill, and the ability to use them effectively in the interests of the client.[3]

2. As members of the legal profession, lawyers hold themselves out as being knowledgeable, skilled and capable in the practice of law. The client is entitled to assume that the lawyer has the ability and capacity to deal adequately with any legal matters undertaken on the client's behalf.[4]

3. The lawyer should not undertake a matter without honestly feeling either competent to handle it, or able to become competent without undue delay, risk or expense to the client. The lawyer who proceeds on any other basis is not being honest with the client. This is an ethical consideration and is to be distinguished from the standard of care that a court would apply for purposes of determining negligence.

4. Competence involves more than an understanding of legal principles: it involves an adequate knowledge of the practice and procedures by which such principles can be effectively applied. To accomplish this the lawyer should keep abreast of developments in all branches of law wherein the

6   *Code of Professional Conduct*

lawyer's practice lies.

5.   In deciding whether the lawyer has employed the requisite degree of knowledge and skill in a particular matter, relevant factors will include the complexity and specialized nature of the matter, the lawyer's general experience, the lawyer's training and experience in the field in question, the preparation and study the lawyer is able to give the matter and whether it is appropriate or feasible to refer the matter to, or associate or consult with, a lawyer of established competence in the field in question. In some circumstances expertise in a particular field of law may be required; often the necessary degree of proficiency will be that of the general practitioner.

Seeking Assistance

6.   The lawyer must be alert to recognize any lack of competence for a particular task and the disservice that would be done the client by undertaking that task. If consulted in such circumstances, the lawyer should either decline to act or obtain the client's instructions to retain, consult or collaborate with a lawyer who is competent in that field. The lawyer should also recognize that competence for a particular task may sometimes require seeking advice from or collaborating with experts in scientific, accounting or other non-legal fields. In such a situation the lawyer should not hesitate to seek the client's instructions to consult experts.

Quality of Service

7.   Numerous examples could be given of conduct that does not meet the quality of service required by the second branch of the Rule. The list that follows is illustrative, but not by any means exhaustive:

- (a) failure to keep the client reasonably informed;
- (b) failure to answer reasonable requests from the client for information;
- (c) unexplained failure to respond to the client's telephone calls;
- (d) failure to keep appointments with clients without explanation or apology;
- (e) informing the client that something will happen or that some step will be taken by a certain date, then letting the date pass without follow-up information or explanation;
- (f) failure to answer within a reasonable time a communication that requires a reply;
- (g) doing the work in hand but doing it so belatedly that its value to the client is diminished or lost;
- (h) slipshod work, such as mistakes or omissions in statements or documents prepared on behalf of the client;
- (i) failure to maintain office staff and facilities adequate to the lawyer's practice;
- (j) failure to inform the client of proposals of settlement, or to explain them properly;

(k) withholding information from the client or misleading the client about the position of a matter in order to cover up the fact of neglect or mistakes;

(l) failure to make a prompt and complete report when the work is finished or, if a final report cannot be made, failure to make an interim report where one might reasonably be expected;

(m) self-induced disability, for example from the use of intoxicants or drugs, which interferes with or prejudices the lawyer's services to the client.[5]

Promptness

8.   The requirement of conscientious, diligent and efficient service means that the lawyer must make every effort to provide prompt service to the client. If the lawyer can reasonably foresee undue delay in providing advice or services, the client should be so informed.[6]

Consequences of Incompetence

9.   It will be observed that the Rule does not prescribe a standard of perfection. A mistake, even though it might be actionable for damages in negligence, would not necessarily constitute a failure to maintain the standard set by the Rule, but evidence of gross neglect in a particular matter or a pattern of neglect or mistakes in different matters may be evidence of such a failure regardless of tort liability. Where both negligence and incompetence are established, while damages may be awarded for the former, the latter can give rise to the additional sanction of disciplinary action.[7]

10.   The lawyer who is incompetent does the client a disservice, brings discredit to the profession, and may bring the administration of justice into disrepute.[8] As well as damaging the lawyer's own reputation and practice, incompetence may also injure the lawyer's associates or dependants.

NOTES

1.   Cf. CBA-COD 2; IBA B-1; ABA-MR 1.1; ABA Canon 6, ECs 6-1 to 6-5, DR 6-101 (A).

"The public looks for a hallmark bestowed by a trusted professional body, and evidenced by entry on a register or members' list (p. 36) ... Having bestowed a hallmark of competence, a professional institute has some responsibility for ensuring that it remains valid.", *Bennion*, p. 48.

See also Bastedo, *A Note on Lawyers' Malpractice*, (1970) 7 Osg. Hall L.J. 311.

2.   As a matter of law, the English and Canadian courts have consistently held that actions by clients against their lawyers for breach of duty stem from the contract of employment made or implied from the retainer, or from the fiduciary relationship that exists between lawyer and client and not on any general tort basis. A contractual or fiduciary relationship must be established: see, e.g., *Groom* v. *Crocker et al.* (1938), 2 All E.R. 394 (C.A.); *Rowswell* v. *Pettit et al.* (1968), 68 D.L.R. (2d) 202 (Ont. H.C.J.) at pp. 209-12 (affd. with variations as to damages, *sub nom. Wilson et al.* v. *Rowswell* (1970)

S.C.R. 865).

3.   "Incompetence goes wider than lack of professional skill, and covers delay, neglect and even sheer disobedience to the client's instructions.", *Bennion,* p. 53.

4.   "This solicitor's very presence as a lawyer . . . is an assurance to the public that he has the training, the talent and the diligence to advise them about their legal rights and competently to aid in their enforcement. Having regard to the faith which a citizen ought to be able to place in a member of the Law Society . . .", per Porter, J.A. in *Cook v. Szott et al.* (1968), 68 D.L.R. (2d) 723 at 726 (Alta. App. Div.).

5.   Cf. *Orkin,* pp. 123-25, and para. 9, *post.*
      "A client has a right to honest explanations for delay on the part of his solicitor, and it is clear that the Benchers . . . concluded that the solicitor had not given an honest explanation for the delay, but on the contrary had deceived his client as to the reason for such delay . . .", per Farris, C.J.S.C. in *Re Legal Professions Act; Sandberg v. "F"* (1945), 4 D.L.R. 446 at 447 (B.C. Visitorial Tribunal).
      Cf. IBA D-1. In some jurisdictions (e.g., Ontario, *Law Society Act,* R.S.O. 1980, c. 233, s. 35) provision is made for inquiry and suspension of members incapacitated by reason of age, physical or mental illness including addiction to alcohol or drugs, or other cause.

6.   For a denunciation of dilatory practices of solicitors, see *Allen* v. *McAlpine et al.* (1968), 2 W.L.R. 366 (C.A.).

7.   "I take the law as to the standard of care of a solicitor to be accurately stated in Charlesworth on Negligence . . . it must be shown that the error or ignorance was such that an ordinary competent solicitor would not have made or shown it", per Lebel, J. in *Aaroe & Aaroe* v. *Seymour* (1957), 6 D.L.R. (2d) 100 at 101 (Ont. H.C.J.).
      "As a future guide to Benchers [this Visitorial Tribunal] expresses the opinion that the words 'good cause' in the *Legal Professions Act* are broad enough . . . to justify the Benchers in suspending a member . . . who has been guilty of a series of acts of gross negligence which, taken together, would amount to a course of conduct sufficient to bring the legal profession into disrepute", per Farris, C.J.S.C. in *Re Legal Professions Act; Baron* v. *"F"* (1945), 4 D.L.R. 525 at 528 (B.C. Visitorial Tribunal).

8.   For an instance of "inordinate and inexcusable delay" see *Tiesmaki* v. *Wilson* (1972), 23 D.L.R. (3d) 179 per Johnson, J.A. at 182 (Alta. App. Div.).

CHAPTER III

ADVISING CLIENTS

RULE

The lawyer must be both honest and candid when advising clients.[1]

Commentary

Scope of Advice

1. The lawyer's duty to the client who seeks legal advice is to give the client a competent opinion based on sufficient knowledge of the relevant facts, an adequate consideration of the applicable law and the lawyer's own experience and expertise. The advice must be open and undisguised, clearly disclosing what the lawyer honestly thinks about the merits and probable results.[2]

2. Whenever it becomes apparent that the client has misunderstood or misconceived what is really involved, the lawyer should explain as well as advise, so that the client is informed of the true position and fairly advised about the real issues or questions involved.[3]

3. The lawyer should clearly indicate the facts, circumstances and assumptions upon which the lawyer's opinion is based, particularly where the circumstances do not justify an exhaustive investigation with resultant expense to the client. However, unless the client instructs otherwise, the lawyer should investigate the matter in sufficient detail to be able to express an opinion rather than merely make comments with many qualifications.

4. The lawyer should be wary of bold and confident assurances to the client, especially when the lawyer's employment may depend upon advising in a particular way.[4]

Second Opinion

5. If the client so desires, the lawyer should assist in obtaining a second opinion.

Compromise or Settlement

6.   The lawyer should advise and encourage the client to compromise or settle a dispute whenever possible on a reasonable basis and should discourage the client from commencing or continuing useless legal proceedings.[5]

Dishonesty or Fraud by Client

7.   When advising the client the lawyer must never knowingly assist in or encourage any dishonesty, fraud, crime or illegal conduct, or instruct the client on how to violate the law and avoid punishment. The lawyer should be on guard against becoming the tool or dupe of an unscrupulous client or of persons associated with such a client.[6]

Test Cases

8.   A *bona fide* test case is not necessarily precluded by the preceding paragraph and, so long as no injury to the person or violence is involved, the lawyer may properly advise and represent a client who, in good faith and on reasonable grounds, desires to challenge or test a law and this can most effectively be done by means of a technical breach giving rise to a test case.[7] In all such situations the lawyer should ensure that the client appreciates the consequences of bringing a test case.

Threatening Criminal Proceedings

9.   Apart altogether from the substantive law on the subject, it is improper for the lawyer to advise, threaten or bring a criminal or quasi-criminal prosecution in order to secure some civil advantage for the client, or to advise, seek or procure the withdrawal of a prosecution in consideration of the payment of money, or transfer of property to, or for the benefit of the client.[8]

Advice on Non-legal matters

10.   In addition to opinions on legal questions, the lawyer may be asked for or expected to give advice on non-legal matters such as the business, policy or social implications involved in a question, or the course the client should choose. In many instances the lawyer's experience will be such that the lawyer's views on non-legal matters will be of real benefit to the client. The lawyer who advises on such matters should, where and to the extent necessary, point out the lawyer's lack of experience or other qualification in the particular field and should clearly distinguish legal advice from such other advice.[9]

Errors and Omissions

11.   The duty to give honest and candid advice requires the lawyer to inform the client promptly of the facts, but without admitting liability, upon discovering that an error or omission has occurred in a matter for

which the lawyer was engaged and that is or may be damaging to the client and cannot readily be rectified. When so informing the client the lawyer should be careful not to prejudice any rights of indemnity that either of them may have under any insurance, client's protection or indemnity plan, or otherwise. At the same time the lawyer should recommend that the client obtain legal advice elsewhere about any rights the client may have arising from such error or omission and whether it is appropriate for the lawyer to continue to act in the matter. The lawyer should also give prompt notice of any potential claim to the lawyer's insurer and any other indemnitor so that any protection from that source will not be prejudiced and, unless the client objects, should assist and co-operate with the insurer or other indemnitor to the extent necessary to enable any claim that is made to be dealt with promptly. If the lawyer is not so indemnified, or to the extent that the indemnity may not fully cover the claim, the lawyer should expeditiously deal with any claim that may be made and must not, under any circumstances, take unfair advantage that might defeat or impair the client's claim. In cases where liability is clear and the insurer or other indemnitor is prepared to pay its portion of the claim, the lawyer is under a duty to arrange for payment of the balance.[10]

Giving Independent Advice

12.   Where the lawyer is asked to provide independent advice or independent representation to another lawyer's client in a situation where a conflict exists, the provision of such advice or representation is an undertaking to be taken seriously and not lightly assumed or perfunctorily discharged. It involves a duty to the client for whom the independent advice or representation is provided that is the same as in any other lawyer and client relationship and ordinarily extends to the nature and result of the transaction.

NOTES

1.   Cf. CBA-COD 3; CBA 3(1); Que. 3.01.01; IBA A-10; *Orkin* at pp. 78-79.
2.   The lawyer should not remain silent when it is plain that the client is rushing into an "unwise, not to say disastrous adventure", per Lord Danckwerts in *Neushal* v. *Mellish & Harkavy* (1967), 111 Sol. Jo. 399 (C.A.).
3.   For cases illustrating the extent to which a lawyer should investigate and verify facts and premises before advising see, e.g., those collected in 43 E. & E.D. (Repl.) at pp. 97-115.
4.   Cf. CBA 3(1) and Eaton, "Practising Ethics" (1966) 9 Can. B.J. 349.
5.   Cf. CBA 3(3) and *Orkin* at pp. 95-97. N.B. C-3: "The lawyer has a duty to discourage a client from commencing useless litigation; but the lawyer is not the judge of his client's case and if there is a reasonable prospect of success the lawyer is justified in proceeding to trial. To avoid needless expense it is the lawyer's duty to investigate and evaluate the proofs or evidence upon which the client relies *before* the institution of proceedings. Similarly, when possible the lawyer must encourage the client to compromise or settle the dispute."

"[The litigation process] operates to bring about a voluntary settlement of a large proportion of disputes . . . . This fact of voluntary settlement is an essential feature of the judicial system", Jackett, C.J.F.C.C., *The Federal Court of Canada, A Manual of Practice* (1971) at pp. 41-42.

6. Cf. CBA 3(5): ". . . the great trust of the lawyer is to be performed within and not without the bounds of the law." See also ABA DR 7-102(A).
    Any complicity such as abetting, counselling or being an accessory to a crime or fraud is obviously precluded.
    Cf. ABA ECs 7-3 and 7-5: "Where the bounds of law are uncertain . . . the two roles [of advocate and adviser] are essentially different. In asserting a position on behalf of his client, an *advocate* for the most part *deals with past conduct* and must take the facts as he finds them. By contrast, a lawyer serving as *adviser* primarily *assists* his client *in determining* the course of *future conduct* and relationships . . . . A lawyer should never encourage or aid his client to commit criminal acts or counsel his client on how to violate the law and avoid punishment . . ." (emphasis added).
    "The arms which [the lawyer] wields are to be the arms of the warrior and not of the assassin. It is his duty to accomplish the interest of his clients *per fas*, but not *per nefas*.", per Cockburn, L.C.J. in a speech in 1864 quoted as being derived from Quintilian in Rogers, "The Ethics of Advocacy" (1899) 15 L.Q.R. 259 at 270-71. Applied to a solicitor in a "very clear case where the solicitor has been guilty of misconduct" and is "floundering in a quagmire of ignorance and moral obliquity" (he having, pending trial of an action and in anticipation of an adverse outcome, advised his client to dispose of its property and, after verdict, taking an assignment of part of that property). *Centre Star* v. *Rossland Miners Union* (1904-05) 11 B.C.R. 194 at 202-03 (B.C. Full Ct.).

7. For example, to challenge the jurisdiction for or the applicability of a shop-closing by-law or a licensing measure, or to determine the rights of a class or group having some common interest.

8. See article, "Criminal Law May Not be Used to Collect Civil Debts" (1968) Vol. 2, No. 4 Law Soc. U.C. Gaz. 36; and cf. B.C. E-5; Alta. 41; ABA DR 7-105(A).

9. Summarized from Johnstone and Hopkins, *Lawyers and Their Work* (1967), Bobbs-Merrill, Indianapolis, pp. 78-81. The lawyer's advice is usually largely based on the lawyer's conception of relevant legal doctrine and its bearing on the particular factual situation at hand. Anticipated reactions of courts, probative value of evidence, the desires and resources of clients, and alternative courses of action are likely to have been considered and referred to. The lawyer may indicate a preference and argue persuasively, or pose available alternatives in neutral terms. The lawyer makes the law and legal processes meaningful to clients; the lawyer explains legal doctrines and practices and their implications; the lawyer interprets both doctrines and impact. Often legal and non-legal issues are intertwined. Much turns on whether the client wants a servant, a critic, a sounding board, a neutral evaluator of ideas, reassurance, authority to strengthen his hand . . . . The real problem may be one, not of role conflict, but of role definition. The lawyer may spot problems of which the client is unaware and call them to his attention.

10. See Bastedo, "A Note on Lawyers' Malpractice" (1970) 7 Osg. Hall L.J. 311.

CHAPTER IV

CONFIDENTIAL INFORMATION

RULE

The lawyer has a duty to hold in strict confidence all information concerning the business and affairs of the client acquired in the course of the professional relationship, and should not divulge such information unless disclosure is expressly or impliedly authorized by the client, required by law[1] or otherwise permitted or required by this Code.

Commentary

Guiding Principles

1. The lawyer cannot render effective professional service to the client unless there is full and unreserved communication between them. At the same time the client must feel completely secure and entitled to proceed on the basis that without any express request or stipulation on the client's part, matters disclosed to or discussed with the lawyer will be held secret and confidential.[2]

2. This ethical rule must be distinguished from the evidentiary rule of lawyer and client privilege with respect to oral or written communications passing between the client and the lawyer. The ethical rule is wider and applies without regard to the nature or source of the information or to the fact that others may share the knowledge.[3]

3. As a general rule, the lawyer should not disclose having been consulted or retained by a person unless the nature of the matter requires such disclosure.

4. The lawyer owes a duty of secrecy to every client without exception, regardless of whether it be a continuing or casual client. The duty survives the professional relationship and continues indefinitely after the lawyer has ceased to act for the client, whether or not differences have arisen between them.[4]

Confidential Information Not to be Used

5.   The fiduciary relationship between lawyer and client forbids the lawyer to use any confidential information covered by the ethical rule for the benefit of the lawyer or a third person, or to the disadvantage of the client. The lawyer who engages in literary works, such as an autobiography, memoirs and the like, should avoid disclosure of confidential information.[5]

6.   The lawyer should take care to avoid disclosure to one client of confidential information concerning or received from another client and should decline employment that might require such disclosure.[6]

7.   The lawyer should avoid indiscreet conversations, even with the lawyer's spouse or family, about a client's affairs and should shun any gossip about such things even though the client is not named or otherwise identified. Likewise the lawyer should not repeat any gossip or information about the client's business or affairs that may be overheard by or recounted to the lawyer. Apart altogether from ethical considerations or questions of good taste, indiscreet shop-talk between lawyers, if overheard by third parties able to identify the matter being discussed, could result in prejudice to the client. Moreover, the respect of the listener for the lawyers concerned and the legal profession generally will probably be lessened.[7]

8.   Although the Rule may not apply to facts that are public knowledge, the lawyer should guard against participating in or commenting upon speculation concerning the client's affairs or business.

Disclosure Authorized by Client

9.   Confidential information may be divulged with the express authority of the client concerned and, in some situations, the authority of the client to divulge may be implied. For example, some disclosure may be necessary in a pleading or other document delivered in litigation being conducted for the client. Again, the lawyer may (unless the client directs otherwise) disclose the client's affairs to partners and associates in the firm and, to the extent necessary, to non-legal staff such as secretaries and filing clerks. This implied authority to disclose places the lawyer under a duty to impress upon associates, students and employees the importance of non-disclosure (both during their employment and afterwards) and requires the lawyer to take reasonable care to prevent their disclosing or using any information that the lawyer is bound to keep in confidence.[8]

Disclosure Where Lawyer's Conduct in Issue

10.   Disclosure may also be justified in order to establish or collect a fee, or to defend the lawyer or the lawyer's associates or employees against any allegation of malpractice or misconduct, but only to the extent necessary for such purposes. (As to potential claims for negligence, see Commentary 10 of the Rule relating to Advising Clients.)[9]

Disclosure to Prevent a Crime

11. Disclosure of information necessary to prevent a crime will be justified if the lawyer has reasonable grounds for believing that a crime is likely to be committed and will be mandatory when the anticipated crime is one involving violence.[10]

12. The lawyer who has reasonable grounds for believing that a dangerous situation is likely to develop at a court facility shall inform the person having responsibility for security at the facility and give particulars. Where possible the lawyer should suggest solutions to the anticipated problem such as:

    (a) the need for further security;

    (b) that judgement be reserved;

    (c) such other measures as may seem advisable.

Disclosure Required by Law

13. When disclosure is required by law or by order of a court of competent jurisdiction, the lawyer should always be careful not to divulge more information than is required.[11]

14. The lawyer who has information known to be confidential government information about a person, acquired when the lawyer was a public officer or employee, shall not represent a client (other than the agency of which the lawyer was a public officer or employee) whose interests are adverse to that person in a matter in which the information could be used to the material disadvantage of that person.

NOTES

1. Cf. CBA-COD 4; CBA 3(7); Que. 3.05.01, .02, .03; Ont. 4; Alta. 15; N.B. C-3; IBA B-8; ABA-MR 1.6; ABA Canon 4, DRs 4-101(A), (B), (C).

2. ". . . [I]t is absolutely necessary that a man, in order to prosecute his rights or defend himself . . . should have recourse to lawyers, and . . . equally necessary . . . that he should be able to place unrestricted and unbounded confidence in the professional agent, and that the communications he so makes to him should be kept secret, unless with his consent (for it is his privilege and not the privilege of the confidential agent) . . .", per Jessell, M.R. in *Anderson* v. *Bank of British Columbia* (1876), L.R. 2 Ch.D. 644 at 649 (C.A.).

3. Cf. *Orkin,* pp. 83-86, and Tollefson, "Privileged Communications in Canada" in Proceedings of 4th Int. Comp. Law Symp. (1967) (Univ. of Ottawa Press) 32 at 36-41.

4. ". . . [A] fundamental rule, namely the duty of a solicitor to refrain from disclosing confidential information unless his client waives the privilege . . . . Because the solicitor owes to his former client a duty to claim the privilege when applicable, it is improper for him not to claim it without showing that it has been properly waived.", per Spence, J. in *Bell et al.* v. *Smith et al.* (1968), S.C.R. 644 at 671. To waive, the client must know of his rights and show a clear intention to forgo them: *Kulchar* v. *March & Benkert* (1950), 1 W.W.R. 272 (Sask. K.B.).

5. Misuse by a lawyer for his own benefit of his client's confidential information may

render the lawyer liable to account: *McMaster* v. *Byrne* (1952), 3 D.L.R. 337 (P.C.); *Bailey* v. *Ornheim* (1962), 40 W.W.R. (N.S.) 129 (B.C.S.C.).

6. *"Joint Retainer.* When two parties employ the *same solicitor,* the rule is that communications passing between either of them and the solicitor, in his *joint capacity,* must be disclosed in favour of the other — e.g., a proposition made by one, to be communicated to the other; or instructions given to the solicitor in the presence of the other; though it is otherwise as to communications made to the solicitor in his *exclusive* capacity." (quotation from *Phipson on Evidence* cited and approved by Atkins, J. in *Chersinoff* v. *Allstate Insurance* (1968), 69 D.L.R. (2d) 653 at 661 (B.C.S.C.).
    As to the duties of lawyers instructed by insurers in the defence of the insured in motor accident cases, see *Groom* v. *Crocker et al.* (1938), 2 All E.R. 394 (C.A.).

7. See Eaton, "Practising Ethics" (1967), 10 Can. B.J. 528.

8. "When a solicitor files an affidavit on behalf of his client . . . it should be assumed, until the contrary is proved, or at least until the solicitor's authority to do so is disputed by the client, that the solicitor has the authority to make the disclosure.", per Lebel, J. in *Kennedy* v. *Diversified* (1949), 1 D.L.R. 59 at 61 (Ont. H.C.).

9. There is no duty or privilege where a client conspires with or deceives his lawyer: *The Queen* v. *Cox* (1885), L.R. 14 Q.B.D. 153 (C.C.R.). Cf. *Orkin* at p. 86 as to the exceptions of crime, fraud and national emergency.

10. To oust privilege the communication must have been made to execute or further a crime or fraud — it must be prospective as distinguished from retrospective: *R.* v. *Bennett* (1964), 41 C.R. 227 (B.C.S.C.) and cases there cited.

11. Cf. Freedman, "Solicitor-Client Privilege Under the Income Tax Act" (1969), 12 Can. B.J. 93.

CHAPTER V

IMPARTIALITY AND CONFLICT OF INTEREST BETWEEN CLIENTS

RULE

The lawyer shall not advise or represent both sides of a dispute and, save after adequate disclosure to and with the consent of the clients or prospective clients concerned, shall not act or continue to act in a matter when there is or is likely to be a conflicting interest.

Commentary

Guiding Principles

1.   A conflicting interest is one that would be likely to affect adversely the lawyer's judgement or advice on behalf of, or loyalty to a client or prospective client.[1]

2.   The reason for the Rule is self-evident. The client or the client's affairs may be seriously prejudiced unless the lawyer's judgement and freedom of action on the client's behalf are as free as possible from compromising influences.[2]

3.   Conflicting interests include, but are not limited to the duties and loyalties of the lawyer or a partner or professional associate of the lawyer to any other client, whether involved in the particular transaction or not, including the obligation to communicate information.[3]

Disclosure of Conflicting Interest

4.   The Rule requires adequate disclosure to enable the client to make an informed decision about whether to have the lawyer act despite the existence or possibility of a conflicting interest. As important as it is to the client that the lawyer's judgement and freedom of action on the client's behalf should not be subject to other interests, duties or obligations, in practice this factor may not always be decisive. Instead it may be only one of several factors that the client will weigh when deciding whether to give the consent referred to in the Rule. Other factors might include, for

example, the availability of another lawyer of comparable expertise and experience, the extra cost, delay and inconvenience involved in engaging another lawyer and the latter's unfamiliarity with the client and the client's affairs. In the result, the client's interests may sometimes be better served by not engaging another lawyer. An example of this sort of situation is when the client and another party to a commercial transaction are continuing clients of the same law firm but are regularly represented by different lawyers in that firm.

5.   Before the lawyer accepts employment from more than one client in the same matter, the lawyer must advise the clients that the lawyer has been asked to act for both or all of them, that no information received in connection with the matter from one can be treated as confidential so far as any of the others is concerned and that, if a dispute develops that cannot be resolved, the lawyer cannot continue to act for both or all of them and may have to withdraw completely. If one of the clients is a person with whom the lawyer has a continuing relationship and for whom the lawyer acts regularly, this fact should be revealed to the other or others at the outset with a recommendation that they obtain independent representation.[4] If, following such disclosure, all parties are content that the lawyer act for them, the lawyer should obtain their consent, preferably in writing, or record their consent in a separate letter to each. The lawyer should, however, guard against acting for more than one client where, despite the fact that all parties concerned consent, it is reasonably obvious that an issue contentious between them may arise or their interests, rights or obligations will diverge as the matter progresses.[5]

6.   If, after the clients involved have consented, an issue contentious between them or some of them arises, the lawyer, although not necessarily precluded from advising them on other non-contentious matters, would be in breach of the Rule if the lawyer attempted to advise them on the contentious issue. In such circumstances the lawyer should ordinarily refer the clients to other lawyers. However, if the issue is one that involves little or no legal advice, for example a business rather than a legal question in a proposed business transaction, and the clients are sophisticated, they may be permitted to settle the issue by direct negotiation in which the lawyer does not participate. Alternatively, the lawyer may refer one client to another lawyer and continue to advise the other if it was agreed at the outset that this course would be followed in the event of a conflict arising.

Lawyer as Arbitrator

7.   The Rule will not prevent a lawyer from arbitrating or settling, or attempting to arbitrate or settle, a dispute between two or more clients or former clients who are *sui juris* and who wish to submit the dispute to the lawyer.[6]

Acting Against Former Client

8.   A lawyer who has acted for a client in a matter should not thereafter act against the client (or against persons who were involved in or associated with the client in that matter) in the same or any related matter, or take a position where the lawyer might be tempted or appear to be tempted to breach the Rule relating to confidential information. It is not, however, improper for the lawyer to act against a former client in a fresh and independent matter wholly unrelated to any work the lawyer has previously done for that person.[7]

9.   For the sake of clarity the foregoing paragraphs are expressed in terms of the individual lawyer and client. However, the term "client" includes a client of the law firm of which the lawyer is a partner or associate, whether or not the lawyer handles the client's work. It also includes the client of a lawyer who is associated with the lawyer in such a manner as to be perceived as practising in partnership or association with the first lawyer, even though in fact no such partnership or association exists.

Acting For More Than One Client

10.   In practice, there are many situations where even though no actual dispute exists between the parties their interests are in conflict. Common examples in a conveyancing practice are vendor and purchaser, or mortgagor and mortgagee. In cases where the lawyer is asked to act for more than one client in such a transaction, the lawyer should recommend that each party be separately represented. In all such transactions the lawyer must observe the rules prescribed by the governing body.

11.   There are also many situations where more than one person may wish to retain the lawyer to handle a transaction and, although their interests appear to coincide, in fact a potential conflict of interest exists. Examples are co-purchasers of real property and persons forming a partnership or corporation. Such cases will be governed by Commentaries 4 and 5 of this Rule.

12.   A lawyer who is employed or retained by an organization represents that organization acting through its duly authorized constituents. In dealing with the organization's directors, officers, employees, members, shareholders or other constituents, the lawyer shall make clear that it is the organization that is the client when it becomes apparent that the organization's interests are adverse to those of the constituents with whom the lawyer is dealing. The lawyer representing an organization may also represent any of the directors, officers, employees, members, shareholders or other constituents, subject to the provisions of this Rule dealing with conflicts of interest.

Burden of Proof

13.   Generally speaking, in disciplinary proceedings arising from a breach

of this Rule the lawyer has the burden of showing good faith and that adequate disclosure was made in the matter and the client's consent was obtained.

NOTES

1. Cf. CBA-COD 5; CBA 3(2), 3(7); Que. 3.05.04; Ont. 5; B.C. B-1, B-2, B-9(b); N.B. C-9; IBA B-7; ABA-MR 1.7, 1.8, 1.9; ABA DRs 5-101(A), 5-105; *Orkin* at pp. 98-101.

2. Cf. ABA EC 5-1.

3. "A solicitor must put at his client's disposal not only his skill but also his knowledge, so far as it is relevant . . . . What he cannot do is to act for the client and at the same time withhold from him any relevant knowledge that he has . . .", per Megarry, J. in *Spector* v. *Ageda* (1971), 3 All E.R. 417 at 430 (Ch. D.).
    "Applying this [*dictum* of Cozens-Hardy, M.R. in *Moody* v. *Cox et al.* (1917), 2 Ch. D. 71] to a simple circumstance which arises in every conveyancing transaction, does a solicitor acting for both parties disclose the previous purchase price to the purchaser . . .? If he does there may be a breach of duty . . . . This example alone faces a solicitor with an unanswerable dilemma, which may only be resolved by his refusing to act for one . . . or . . . possibly stepping back from a situation in which both clients really need positive advice.", article in (1970) Law Soc. Gazette 332; and see thirteen examples of difficulties there listed. In *Cornell* v. *Jaeger* (1968), 63 W.W.R. 747 (Man.) the non-disclosure by a solicitor of his personal interest in a property to the clear detriment of his client was held to amount to fraud.

4. "Notwithstanding that [the solicitor] had acted for the plaintiff and had been introduced to the defendants by the plaintiff and acted for both the plaintiff and R while they were negotiating the purchase . . . he divorced himself from his responsibilities . . . and acted for the defendants while they acquired the property . . . and, after the writ was issued . . . acted for both defendants . . . . I refer to *Bowstead on Agency*: 'It is the duty of a solicitor . . . (8) not to act for the opponent of his client, of or a former client, in any case in which his knowledge of the affairs of such client or former client will give him an undue advantage . . .' *This is a principle of ethical standards which admits to no fine distinctions but should be applied in its broadest sense,* and it makes no difference whether the solicitor was first acting for two parties jointly who subsequently disagreed and became involved over the subject-matter of his joint retainer, or acted for one party with respect to a matter and took up a case for another party against his former client about the same matter.", per McRuer, C.J.H.C. in *Sinclair* v. *Ridout & Moran* (1955), 1 O.R. 167 at 182-83 (Ont. H.C.) (emphasis added). See Knepper, "Conflicts of Interest in Defending Insurance Cases" (1970), Defence L.J. 515, and "Guiding Principles", *ibid.,* pp. 540-44.

5. Cf. Ont. 5(5). Common "multiple client" situations where there is real danger of divergence of interest arising between clients include the defending of co-accused, the representation of co-plaintiffs in tort cases or of insureds and their insurers, the representation of classes or groups such as beneficiaries under a will or trust and construction lien and bankruptcy claimants.
    See for examples *Orkin* at p. 100.
    [Leave to appeal granted] ". . . by reason of the same solicitor appearing for R and D, and it being apparent that there was a conflict of interest between R and D, each one blaming the other for the injuries of the children, he should not have acted for D after having acted for R.", *Regina* v. *De Patie* (1971), 1 O.R. 698 at 699

(Ont. C.A.).

6.   Cf. Que. 55; ABA 5-20.

7.   "The appellant had for many years been the respondent's solicitor, and a quarrel . . . brought about a rupture . . . . It was then . . . that the appellant by his letters to the wife incited her and improperly encouraged her to prosecute an action . . . thus stirring up a litigation against the respondent.", per Taschereau, J. in *Sheppard* v. *Frind* (1941), S.C.R. 531 at 535 (S.C.C.).
    "The solicitor acting for the defendant . . . drew the mortgage and advised the said defendant on the effect thereof. Later the same solicitor acting for the mortgagee bank brought action against his former client based on a claim arising out of and related to that mortgage. Solicitors should not so conduct themselves even with the knowledge and consent of all parties . . .", *La Banque Provinciale* v. *Adjutor Levesque Roofing* (1968), 68 D.L.R. (2d) 340 at 345 (N.B.C.A.).

CHAPTER VI

CONFLICT OF INTEREST
BETWEEN LAWYER AND CLIENT

RULE

(a) The lawyer should not enter into a business transaction with the client or knowingly give to or acquire from the client an ownership, security or other pecuniary interest unless:
  (i)   the transaction is a fair and reasonable one and its terms are fully disclosed to the client in writing in a manner that is reasonably understood by the client;
  (ii) the client is given a reasonable opportunity to seek independent legal advice about the transaction, the onus being on the lawyer to prove that the client's interests were protected by such independent advice; and
  (iii) the client consents in writing to the transaction.

(b) The lawyer shall not enter into or continue a business transaction with the client if:
  (i)   the client expects or might reasonably be assumed to expect that the lawyer is protecting the client's interests;
  (ii) there is a significant risk that the interests of the lawyer and the client may differ.

(c) The lawyer shall not act for the client where the lawyer's duty to the client and the personal interests of the lawyer or an associate are in conflict.

(d) The lawyer shall not prepare an instrument giving the lawyer or an associate a substantial gift from the client, including a testamentary gift.

Commentary

Guiding Principles

1. The principles enunciated in the Rule relating to impartiality and conflict of interest between clients apply *mutatis mutandis* to this Rule.

2. A conflict of interest between lawyer and client exists in all cases where the lawyer gives property to or acquires it from the client by way of

purchase, gift, testamentary disposition or otherwise. Such transactions are to be avoided. When they are contemplated, the prudent course is to insist that the client either be independently represented or have independent legal advice.

3.   This Rule applies also to situations involving associates of the lawyer. Associates of the lawyer within the meaning of the Rule include the lawyer's spouse, children, any relative of the lawyer (or of the lawyer's spouse) living under the same roof, any partner or associate of the lawyer in the practice of law, a trust or estate in which the lawyer has a substantial beneficial interest or for which the lawyer acts as a trustee or in a similar capacity, and a corporation of which the lawyer is a director or in which the lawyer or an associate owns or controls, directly or indirectly, a significant number of shares.[1]

Debtor-Creditor Relationship to be Avoided

4.   The lawyer should avoid entering into a debtor-creditor relationship with the client. The lawyer should not borrow money from a client who is not in the business of lending money.[2] It is undesirable that the lawyer lend money to the client except by way of advancing necessary expenses in a legal matter that the lawyer is handling for the client.

Joint Ventures

5.   The lawyer who has a personal interest in a joint business venture with others may represent or advise the business venture in legal matters between it and third parties, but should not represent or advise either the joint business venture or the joint venturers in respect of legal matters as between them.

When Person to be Considered a Client

6.   The question of whether a person is to be considered a client of the lawyer when such person is lending money to the lawyer, or buying, selling, making a loan to or investment in, or assuming an obligation in respect of a business, security or property in which the lawyer or an associate of the lawyer has an interest, or in respect of any other transaction, is to be determined having regard to all the circumstances. A person who is not otherwise a client may be deemed to be a client for purposes of this Rule if such person might reasonably feel entitled to look to the lawyer for guidance and advice in respect of the transaction. In those circumstances the lawyer must consider such person to be a client and will be bound by the same fiduciary obligations that attach to a lawyer in dealings with a client. The onus shall be on the lawyer to establish that such a person was not in fact looking to the lawyer for guidance and advice.

NOTES

1.   Cf. ABA-COD 5. As to corporations, cf. ABA-MR 1.13; ABA EC 5-18: "A lawyer employed or retained by a corporation or similar entity owes his allegiance to the entity and not to a stockholder, director, officer, employee, representative, or other person connected with the entity. In advising the entity, a lawyer should keep paramount its interests . . .".

2.   Cf. Ont. 5; Alta. 34; and B.C. B-13: ". . . in a number of instances of professional misconduct . . . the borrowing of money by [the lawyers] in question has been a factor leading to the . . . misconduct. [A lawyer] should not borrow money from his clients save in exceptional circumstances, and in that case the onus of proving that the client's interests were fully protected by the nature of the case or by independent legal advice will rest upon [the lawyer] . . . . [Attention is called to] the various transactions and dealings that the courts have held to be improper or reprehensible conduct in violation of these principles, and which, in addition to their consequences at law, constitute professional misconduct."
Cf. ABA EC 5-8.

CHAPTER VII

OUTSIDE INTERESTS AND
THE PRACTICE OF LAW

RULE

The lawyer who engages in another profession, business or occupation concurrently with the practice of law must not allow such outside interest to jeopardize the lawyer's professional integrity, independence or competence.[1]

Commentary

Guiding Principles

1. The term "outside interest" covers the widest possible range and includes activities that may overlap or be connected with the practice of law, such as engaging in the mortgage business, acting as a director of a client corporation, or writing on legal subjects, as well as activities not so connected such as a career in business, politics, broadcasting or the performing arts. In each case the question of whether the lawyer may properly engage in the outside interest and to what extent the lawyer will be subject to any applicable law or rule of the governing body.[2]

2. Whenever an overriding social, political, economic or other consideration arising from the outside interest might influence the lawyer's judgement, the lawyer should be governed by the considerations declared in the Rule relating to conflict of interest between lawyer and client.[3]

3. Where the outside interest is in no way related to the legal services being performed for clients, ethical considerations will usually not arise unless the lawyer's conduct brings either the lawyer or the profession into disrepute,[4] or impairs the lawyer's competence as, for example, where the outside interest occupies so much time that clients suffer because of the lawyer's lack of attention or preparation.

4. The lawyer must not carry on, manage or be involved in any outside business, investment, property or occupation in such a way that makes it difficult to distinguish in which capacity the lawyer is acting in a particular

transaction, or that would give rise to a conflict of interest or duty to a client.[5] When acting or dealing in respect of a transaction involving an outside interest in a business, investment, property or occupation, the lawyer must disclose any personal interest, must declare to all parties in the transaction or to their solicitors whether the lawyer is acting on the lawyer's own behalf or in a professional capacity or otherwise, and must adhere throughout the transaction to standards of conduct as high as those that this Code requires of a lawyer engaged in the practice of law.

5.   The lawyer who has an outside interest in a business, investment, property or occupation:

    (a)   must not be identified as a lawyer when carrying on, managing or being involved in such outside interest; and

    (b)   must ensure that monies received in respect of the day-to-day carrying on, operation and management of such outside interest are deposited in an account other than the lawyer's trust account, unless such monies are received by the lawyer when acting in a professional capacity as a lawyer on behalf of the outside interest.

6.   In order to be compatible with the practice of law the other profession, business or occupation:

    (a)   must be an honourable one that does not detract from the status of the lawyer or the legal profession generally; and

    (b)   must not be such as would likely result in a conflict of interest between the lawyer and a client.

NOTES

1.   Cf. CBA-COD 6; B.C. B-8; N.B. F-3; IBA D-1. This Rule is closely connected with the Rule relating to conflict of interest between lawyer and client.

2.   In Quebec, s. 122(1)(b) of the *Bar Act* provides that a person shall become disqualified from practising as an advocate when "he holds a position or an office incompatible with the practice or dignity of the profession of advocate."
Sask. 7 and Que. 4.01.01(c) prohibit lawyers from having an interest in collection agencies. Cf. *Orkin* at pp. 188-90.

3.   B.C. B-8 identifies the dangers ". . . that make it difficult for a client to distinguish in which capacity [the lawyer] is acting in a particular instance or which could give rise to a conflict of interest or duty to a client."
For a discussion of "independent judgment" as it may be impaired by outside interests, see Weddington, "A Fresh Approach to Independent Judgment" (1969) 11 Ariz. L.R. 31.

4.   In *Re Weare* (1893), 2 Q.B. 439 (C.A.) the striking off of a solicitor who had knowingly rented his premises for use as a brothel was sustained by the court.

5.   Further examples of outside interests that could, unless clearly disclosed and defined, confuse or mislead persons dealing with a lawyer engaging in them include:
- professions such as accountancy and engineering;
- occupations such as those of merchant, land developer or speculator, building

contractor, real estate, insurance or financial agent, broker, financier, property manager, or public relations adviser.

CHAPTER VIII

PRESERVATION OF CLIENTS' PROPERTY

RULE

The lawyer owes a duty to the client to observe all relevant laws and rules respecting the preservation and safekeeping of the client's property entrusted to the lawyer. Where there are no such laws or rules, or the lawyer is in any doubt, the lawyer should take the same care of such property as a careful and prudent owner would when dealing with property of like description.[1]

Commentary

Guiding Principles

1. The lawyer's duties with respect to safekeeping, preserving and accounting for the clients' monies and other property are generally the subject of special rules.[2] In the absence of such rules the lawyer should adhere to the minimum standards set out in the note.[3] "Property", apart from clients' monies, includes securities such as mortgages, negotiable instruments, stocks, bonds, etc., original documents such as wills, title deeds, minute books, licences, certificates, etc., other papers such as clients' correspondence files, reports, invoices, etc., as well as chattels such as jewelry, silver, etc.[4]

2. The lawyer should promptly notify the client upon receiving any property of or relating to the client unless satisfied that the client knows that it has come into the lawyer's custody.[5]

3. The lawyer should clearly label and identify the client's property and place it in safekeeping separate and apart from the lawyer's own property.

4. The lawyer should maintain adequate records of clients' property in the lawyer's custody so that it may be promptly accounted for, or delivered to, or to the order of, the client upon request. The lawyer should ensure that such property is delivered to the right person and, in case of dispute as to the person entitled, may have recourse to the courts.[6]

5. The duties here expressed are closely related to those concerning confidential information.[7] The lawyer should keep clients' papers and

other property out of sight as well as out of reach of those not entitled to see them and should, subject to any right of lien,[8] return them promptly to the clients upon request or at the conclusion of the lawyer's retainer.

Privilege

6.   The lawyer should be alert to claim on behalf of clients any lawful privilege respecting information about their affairs, including their files and property if seized or attempted to be seized by a third party. In this regard the lawyer should be familiar with the nature of clients' privilege, and with relevant statutory provisions such as those in the *Income Tax Act*,[9] the *Criminal Code*, the *Canadian Charter of Rights and Freedoms* and other statutes.

NOTES

1.   Cf. CBA-COD 7; CBA 3 (8); Que. 3.02.06; ABA-MR 1.15; ABA DR 9-102(B). Although the basic duty here declared may parallel the legal duty under the law of bailment, it is reiterated as being a matter of professional responsibility quite apart from the position in law.

2.   For example, in Ontario, secs. 13 to 18 captioned "Books, Records and Accounts" of O.Reg. 573 enacted pursuant to the *Law Society Act*, R.S.O. 1980, c. 233. Similar provisions exist in the other provinces and territories.

3.   The minimum standards are:
      (a)   paying into and keeping monies received or held by the lawyer for or on behalf of clients in a trust bank account or accounts separate from the bank account of the lawyer or the lawyer's firm;
      (b)   keeping properly written books and accounts of all monies received, held or paid by the lawyer for or on behalf of each of the lawyer's clients which clearly distinguish such monies from the monies of every other client and from the monies of the lawyer and the lawyer's firm;
      (c)   not retaining for an unnecessarily long period, without the express authority of the client, monies received for or on behalf of such client;
      (d)   subject to rules prescribed by the governing body of the province, no lawyer shall take fees, as opposed to disbursements, from funds held in trust for a client without the client's express authority unless the work being done by the lawyer for the client has been performed and a proper account in respect thereof has been rendered to the client. Where a client authorizes the payment of fees from trust funds before an account has been rendered, this arrangement should be recorded in writing and an interim account sent to the client forthwith;
      (e)   the lawyer should not estimate a lump sum that may in the aggregate be owed by a number of clients and then transfer that sum in bulk from a trust account to the lawyer's general account without allocating specific amounts to each client and rendering an account to each client.

4.   In some provinces statutes authorize the depositing of valuable documents with public officials for safekeeping. As to wills, see *Comment* in (1970) 4 Law Soc. U.C. Gaz. 117.

5.   Cf. ABA DR 9-102 (B)(1).

6.   For example, by seeking leave to interplead.

7.   Cf. the Rule relating to confidential information.

8.   Cf. para. 10 of the Rule relating to withdrawal. As to the proper disposition of papers, which is frequently a perplexing problem, see *Cordery on Solicitors* (6th ed. 1968) at pp. 118-20 for a discussion of law and principles and a table of categories with supporting authorities.

The lawyer's arrangements and procedures for the storage and eventual destruction of completed files should reflect the foregoing considerations and particularly the continuing obligation as to confidentiality.

Further, statutes such as the *Income Tax Act* and the operation of limitations statutes pertinent to the client's position may preclude the destruction of files or particular papers. In several provinces statutes provide for the appointment of a custodian or trustee or the intervention of the syndic to conserve clients' property where a lawyer has died, absconded or become incapable. See, e.g., *Barristers and Solicitors Act*, R.S.B.C. 1979, c. 26, s. 69; *Bar Act,* R.S.Q. 1977, c. B-1, s. 76(2); *Law Society Act*, R.S.O. 1980, c. 233, s. 43.

9.   See Freedman, "Solicitor-Client Privilege under the Income Tax Act" (1969) 12 Can. B.J. 93.

CHAPTER IX

THE LAWYER AS ADVOCATE

RULE

When acting as an advocate, the lawyer must treat the tribunal with courtesy and respect and must represent the client resolutely, honourably and within the limits of the law.[1]

Commentary

Guiding Principles

1. The advocate's duty to the client "fearlessly to raise every issue, advance every argument, and ask every question, however distasteful, which he thinks will help his client's case" and to endeavour "to obtain for his client the benefit of any and every remedy and defence which is authorized by law"[2] must always be discharged by fair and honourable means, without illegality and in a manner consistent with the lawyer's duty to treat the court with candour, fairness, courtesy and respect.[3]

Prohibited Conduct

2. The lawyer must not, for example:
    (a) abuse the process of the tribunal by instituting or prosecuting proceedings that, although legal in themselves, are clearly motivated by malice on the part of the client and are brought solely for the purpose of injuring another party;[4]
    (b) knowingly assist or permit the client to do anything that the lawyer considers to be dishonest or dishonourable;[5]
    (c) appear before a judicial officer when the lawyer, the lawyer's associates or the client have business or personal relationships with such officer that give rise to real or apparent pressure, influence or inducement affecting the impartiality of such officer;[6]
    (d) attempt or allow anyone else to attempt, directly or indirectly, to influence the decision or actions of a tribunal or any of its officials by any means except open persuasion as an advocate;[7]
    (e) knowingly attempt to deceive or participate in the deception of

a tribunal or influence the course of justice by offering false evidence, misstating facts or law, presenting or relying upon a false or deceptive affidavit, suppressing what ought to be disclosed or otherwise assisting in any fraud, crime or illegal conduct;[8]

(f) knowingly misstate the contents of a document, the testimony of a witness, the substance of an argument or the provisions of a statute or like authority;[9]

(g) knowingly assert something for which there is no reasonable basis in evidence, or the admissibility of which must first be established;[10]

(h) deliberately refrain from informing the tribunal of any pertinent adverse authority that the lawyer considers to be directly in point and that has not been mentioned by an opponent;[11]

(i) dissuade a material witness from giving evidence, or advise such a witness to be absent;[12]

(j) knowingly permit a witness to be presented in a false or misleading way or to impersonate another;

(k) needlessly abuse, hector or harass a witness;

(l) needlessly inconvenience a witness.

Errors and Omissions

3.   The lawyer who has unknowingly done or failed to do something that, if done or omitted knowingly, would have been in breach of this Rule and discovers it, has a duty to the court, subject to the Rule relating to confidential information, to disclose the error or omission and do all that can reasonably be done in the circumstances to rectify it.[13]

Duty to Withdraw

4.   If the client wishes to adopt a course that would involve a breach of this Rule, the lawyer must refuse and do everything reasonably possible to prevent it. If the client persists in such a course the lawyer should, subject to the Rule relating to withdrawal, withdraw or seek leave of the court to do so.[14]

The Lawyer as Witness

5.   The lawyer who appears as an advocate should not submit the lawyer's own affidavit to or testify before a tribunal save as permitted by local rule or practice, or as to purely formal or uncontroverted matters. This also applies to the lawyer's partners and associates; generally speaking, they should not testify in such proceedings except as to merely formal matters. The lawyer should not express personal opinions or beliefs, or assert as fact anything that is properly subject to legal proof, cross-examination or challenge. The lawyer must not in effect become an unsworn witness or put the lawyer's own credibility in issue. The lawyer who is a necessary witness should testify and entrust the conduct of the

case to someone else. Similarly, the lawyer who was a witness in the proceedings should not appear as advocate in any appeal from the decision in those proceedings.[15] There are no restrictions upon the advocate's right to cross-examine another lawyer, and the lawyer who does appear as a witness should not expect to receive special treatment by reason of professional status.

Interviewing Witnesses

6. The lawyer may properly seek information from any potential witness (whether under subpoena or not) but should disclose the lawyer's interest and take care not to subvert or suppress any evidence or procure the witness to stay out of the way.[16] The lawyer shall not approach or deal with an opposite party who is professionally represented save through or with the consent of that party's lawyer.[17]

Unmeritorious Proceedings

7. The lawyer should never waive or abandon the client's legal rights (for example an available defence under a statute of limitations) without the client's informed consent. In civil matters it is desirable that the lawyer should avoid and discourage the client from resorting to frivolous or vexatious objections or attempts to gain advantage from slips or oversights not going to the real merits, or tactics that will merely delay or harass the other side. Such practices can readily bring the administration of justice and the legal profession into disrepute.[18]

Encouraging Settlements

8. Whenever the case can be settled fairly, the lawyer should advise and encourage the client to do so rather than commence or continue legal proceedings.[19]

Duties of Prosecutor

9. When engaged as a prosecutor, the lawyer's prime duty is not to seek a conviction, but to present before the trial court all available credible evidence relevant to the alleged crime in order that justice may be done through a fair trial upon the merits.[20] The prosecutor exercises a public function involving much discretion and power and must act fairly and dispassionately. The prosecutor should not do anything that might prevent the accused from being represented by counsel or communicating with counsel and, to the extent required by law and accepted practice, should make timely disclosure to the accused or defence counsel (or to the court if the accused is not represented) of all relevant facts and known witnesses, whether tending to show guilt or innocence, or that would affect the punishment of the accused.[21]

Duties of Defence Counsel

10. When defending an accused person, the lawyer's duty is to protect the

client as far as possible from being convicted except by a court of competent jurisdiction and upon legal evidence sufficient to support a conviction for the offence charged. Accordingly, and notwithstanding the lawyer's private opinion as to credibility or merits, the lawyer may properly rely upon all available evidence or defences including so-called technicalities not known to be false or fraudulent.[22]

11. Admissions made by the accused to the lawyer may impose strict limitations on the conduct of the defence and the accused should be made aware of this. For example, if the accused clearly admits to the lawyer the factual and mental elements necessary to constitute the offence, the lawyer, if convinced that the admissions are true and voluntary, may properly take objection to the jurisdiction of the court, or to the form of the indictment, or to the admissibility or sufficiency of the evidence, but must not suggest that some other person committed the offence, or call any evidence that, by reason of the admissions, the lawyer believes to be false. Nor may the lawyer set up an affirmative case inconsistent with such admissions, for example, by calling evidence in support of an alibi intended to show that the accused could not have done, or in fact had not done, the act. Such admissions will also impose a limit upon the extent to which the lawyer may attack the evidence for the prosecution. The lawyer is entitled to test the evidence given by each individual witness for the prosecution and argue that the evidence taken as a whole is insufficient to amount to proof that the accused is guilty of the offence charged, but the lawyer should go no further than that.[23]

Agreement on Guilty Plea

12. Where, following investigation,
  (a) the defence lawyer *bona fide* concludes and advises the accused client that an acquittal of the offence charged is uncertain or unlikely,
  (b) the client is prepared to admit the necessary factual and mental elements,
  (c) the lawyer fully advises the client of the implications and possible consequences of a guilty plea and that the matter of sentence is solely in the discretion of the trial judge, and
  (d) the client so instructs the lawyer, preferably in writing,

it is proper for the lawyer to discuss and agree tentatively with the prosecutor to enter a plea of guilty on behalf of the client to the offence charged or to a lesser or included offence or to another offence appropriate to the admissions, and also on a disposition or sentence to be proposed to the court. The public interest and the client's interests must not, however, be compromised by agreeing to a guilty plea.[24]

Undertakings

13. An undertaking given by the lawyer to the court or to another lawyer in the course of litigation or other adversary proceedings must be strictly

and scrupulously carried out. Unless clearly qualified in writing, the lawyer's undertaking is a personal promise and responsibility.[25]

Courtesy

14. The lawyer should at all times be courteous and civil to the court and to those engaged on the other side. Legal contempt of court and the professional obligation outlined here are not identical, and a consistent pattern of rude, provocative or disruptive conduct by the lawyer, even though unpunished as contempt, might well merit disciplinary action.[26]

Role in Adversary Proceedings

15. In adversary proceedings, the lawyer's function as advocate is openly and necessarily partisan. Accordingly, the lawyer is not obliged (save as required by law or under paragraphs 2(h) or 7 above) to assist an adversary or advance matters derogatory to the client's case. When opposing interests are not represented, for example in *ex parte* or uncontested matters, or in other situations where the full proof and argument inherent in the adversary system cannot be obtained, the lawyer must take particular care to be accurate, candid and comprehensive in presenting the client's case so as to ensure that the court is not misled.[27]

Communicating with Witnesses

16. When in court the lawyer should observe local rules and practices concerning communication with a witness about the witness's evidence or any issue in the proceeding. Generally, it is considered improper for counsel who called a witness to communicate with that witness without leave of the court while such witness is under cross-examination.[28]

Agreements Guaranteeing Recovery

17. In civil proceedings the lawyer has a duty not to mislead the court about the position of the client in the adversary process. Thus, where a lawyer representing a client in litigation has made or is party to an agreement made before or during the trial whereby a plaintiff is guaranteed recovery by one or more parties notwithstanding the judgement of the court, the lawyer shall disclose full particulars of the agreement to the court and all other parties.[29]

Scope of the Rule

18. The principles of this Rule apply generally to the lawyer as advocate and therefore extend not only to court proceedings but also to appearances and proceedings before boards, administrative tribunals and other bodies, regardless of their function or the informality of their procedures.[30]

NOTES

1. Cf. CBA-COD 8; CBA 2(1), 3(5); ABA-MR 3; ABA Canon 7.
    "The concept that counsel is the mouth-piece of his client and that his speech is the speech of the client is as unfortunate as it is inaccurate. He is not the agent or delegate of his client. Within proper bounds, however, counsel must be fearless and independent in the defence of his client's rights . . . . He must be completely selfless in standing up courageously for his client's rights, and he should never expose himself to the reproach that he has sacrificed his client's interests on the altar of expediency . . .", per Schroeder, J.A., "Some Ethical Problems in Criminal Law" in Law Soc. U.C. Special Lectures (1963) 87 at 102.

2. The sources of the quotations are (a) per Lord Reid in *Rondel* v. *Worsley* (1969), 1 A.C. 191 at 227 and (b) CBA 3(5).

3. Cf. CBA 3(5). ". . . [H]e must be a man of character. The Court must be able to rely on the advocate's word; his word must indeed be his bond . . . . The advocate has a duty to his client, a duty to the Court, and a duty to the State; but he has above all a duty to himself that he shall be, as far as it lies in his power, a man of integrity. No profession calls for higher standards of honour and uprightness, and no profession, perhaps offers greater temptations to forsake them . . .", from Hyde, *Lord Birkett* (1964, Hamish Hamilton, London) at p. 551. Courtesy and respect, as used herein, include the duty to be prompt and punctual.

4. Cf. IBA A-19; ABA DR 7-102 (A)(1).

5. Cf. IBA A-15.

6. Cf. ABA Canon 9, DR 9-101; IBA E-3.

7. Cf. CBA 2(4), 5(5); Que. 2.03, 3.05; N.B. B-6; ABA 9 ECs 7-34 and 7-35, DR 7-110; IBA A-16.
    In *Toronto Transit* v. *Aqua Taxi* (1955) O.W.N. 857 (Ont. H.C.), where a sealed letter improperly attempting to influence a decision had been delivered to a judge, the Court, while exonerating the lawyers concerned, made it clear that any involvement in such conduct would be most improper.

8. Where a lawyer joined in a scheme to mislead the Court by arranging proceedings to result in an apparent acquittal which could then be used to answer prior pending proceedings for the same offence (a justice, a constable and another lawyer being misled in the process), the Court said: "These facts establish a stupid, but nevertheless unworthy, attempt to pervert the course of justice, and most certainly constitute conduct unbecoming a barrister and solicitor in the pursuit of his profession.", *Banks* v. *Hall* (1941), 2 W.W.R. 534 (Sask. C.A.).
    A lawyer counselling false evidence would be guilty of perjury if it were given (*Criminal Code*, ss. 22, 120), and of counselling if it were not (*ibid.*, s. 422).
    It is an offence to fabricate anything with intent that it be used as evidence by any means other than perjury or incitement to perjury (*ibid.*, s. 125).
    Similarly, it is an offence wilfully to attempt in any manner to obstruct, pervert or defeat the course of justice (*ibid.*, s. 127).
    "The swearing of an untrue affidavit . . . is perhaps the most obvious example of conduct which a solicitor cannot knowingly permit . . . . He cannot properly, still less can he consistently with his duty to the Court, prepare and place a perjured affidavit upon file . . . . A solicitor who has innocently put on the file an affidavit by his client which he has subsequently discovered to be certainly false owes it to the Court to put the matter right at the earliest date if he continues to act . . .". per Viscount Maugham in *Myers* v. *Elman* (1940), A.C. 282 at 293-94 (H.L.).
    "[Counsel] had full knowledge of the impropriety of the paragraphs in the affidavit . . . [and] is bound to accept responsibility for [them] . . . . If he knows that his client is making false statements under oath and does nothing to correct it,

his silence indicates, at the very least, a gross neglect of duty.", per McLennan, J.A. in *Re Ontario Crime Commission* (1962), 37 D.L.R. (2d) 382 at 391 (Ont. C.A.).

9. Cf. N.B. B-1; IBA A-14; ABA DR 7-102 (A) (5).

10. Cf. N.B. B-7; ABA EC 7-25; DR 7-106 (C) (1).

11. Cf. CBA 1(1); N.B. B-3; IBA A-14; ABA EC 7-23, DR 7-106 (B) (1).
See *Glebe Sugar* v. *Greenock Trustees* (1921), W.N. 85 (H.L.) for a strong statement by Lord Birkenhead on the duty of counsel to disclose to the court authorities bearing one way or the other: "The extreme impropriety of such a course [withholding a known pertinent authority] could not be made too plain." See also *Plant* v. *Urquhart* (1922), 1 W.W.R. 632 (B.C.C.A.) per McPhillips, J. at 638-39.

12. Cf. IBA A-18; ABA DR 7-109(B).

13. Cf. N.B. B-8; ABA DRs 7-102(B) and 4-101(C) (2).

14. Cf. ABA DR 2-110(B) (2); N.B. B-8: "Upon learning of fraudulent testimony participated in by his client, counsel has a duty to withdraw from the case and to advise the court and the adverse party of the fraud." See also *Orkin* at p. 127.

15. Cf. CBA 2(3); N.B. C-11; ABA EC 7-24, DR 7-106 (C) (3), (4).
"It is to be borne in mind that the function of counsel in any Court is that of an advocate; he is there to plead his client's cause upon the record before the Court and he does not in any sense occupy the dual position of advocate and witness.", per McGillivray, J.A. in *Cairns* v. *Cairns* (1931), 3 W.W.R. 335 at 345 (Alta. App. Div.).
"It is improper, in my opinion, for Counsel for the Crown to express his opinion as to the guilt or innocence of the accused. In the article to which I have referred it is said that it is because the character or eminence of a counsel is to be wholly disregarded in determining the justice or otherwise of his client's cause that it is an inflexible rule of forensic pleading that an advocate shall not, as such, express his personal opinion of or his belief in his client's cause.", per Locke, J. in *Boucher* v. *The Queen* (1955), S.C.R. 16 at 26.
As to the impropriety of a lawyer witness later appearing as counsel, see *Imperial Oil* v. *Grabarchuk* (1974), 3 O.R. (3d) 783 (Ont. C.A.); *Phoenix* v. *Metcalfe* (1974), 5 W.W.R. 661 (B.C.C.A.).

16. Cf. B.C. D-1 (b); N.B. B-8; IBA A-18; ABA DR 7-109(A), (B), (C). "I do not know of any rule that a defence counsel cannot interview a witness that may be called for the Crown . . . . The Crown, by issuing a lot of subpoenas, cannot throw a cloud over a lot of witnesses, excluding the defence from the preparation of their case.", per Roach, J.A. in *R.* v. *Gibbons* (1946), 86 C.C.C. 20 at 28-29 (Ont. C.A.).

17. Cf. B.C. D-1(b); N.B. D-7, D-8; ABA EC 7-19, DR 7-104(A)(1).
B.C. D-1(b) discusses situations where it is difficult to tell whether one is dealing with a witness (which is proper) or communicating with an opposite party who is legally represented (which is improper). The problem may arise where the opposite party is a corporation or government agency. The test suggested is: "Is he likely to be involved in the decision-making process of the party, or does he merely carry out the directions of others?"
"The principle was laid down long ago . . . that once it appears a person has an attorney there can be no effective dealing except through him." ". . . [A] lawyer 'should never in any way . . . attempt to negotiate or compromise the matter directly with any party represented by a lawyer, except *through* such lawyer' . . . . To notify the lawyer that the matter is settled is not to negotiate through him". per J.A. in *Nelson* v. *Murphy* (1957), 22 W.W.R. 137 at 142 (Man. C.A.).

18. Cf. CBA 4(4); N.B. D-4; ABA ECs 7-38, 7-39, DR 7-106(C)(5). See *Orkin* at pp.

60-63 for instances of dilatory tactics held to be improper.

19. Cf. CBA 3(3); *Orkin* at pp. 95-97; and see paragraph 5 of the Rule relating to advising clients.

20. But see para. 10, *post.*

21. Cf. CBA 1(2); N.B. C-12; ABA ECs 7-13, 7-14, DR 7-103; *Orkin* at pp. 116-20. "It cannot be overemphasized that the purpose of a criminal prosecution is not to obtain a conviction, it is to lay before the jury what the Crown considers to be credible evidence relevant to what is alleged to be a crime. Counsel have a duty to see that all available legal proof of the facts is presented; it should be done firmly and pressed to its legitimate strength but it must also be done fairly. The role of prosecutor excludes any notion of winning or losing; his function is a matter of public duty than which in civil life there can be none charged with greater personal responsibility. It is to be performed with an ingrained sense of the dignity, the seriousness and the justness of judicial proceedings.", per Rand, J. in *Boucher* v. *The Queen* (1955), S.C.R. 16 at 23-24.
See also *Richard* v. *The Queen* (1960), 126 C.C.C. 255 per Bridges, J.A. at p. 280; *Regina* v. *Lalonde* (1972), 5 C.C.C. (2d) 168; and Martin, "Preparation for Trial", Law Soc. U.C. Special Lectures (1969) p. 221 at 235 *et seq.*

22. Cf. CBA 2(6); N.B. C-6; IBA B-5; ABA EC 7-24, DR 7-106(C)(4).

23. See *Orkin,* p. 115, and Boulton, *Conduct and Etiquette at the Bar,* pp. 71-73, reproducing the substance of 1912 Annual Statement of the General Council of the Bar; also quoted and commented on by Schroeder, J.A., *supra,* note 1, at pp. 94-97.
See also Martin, "The Role and Responsibility of the Defence Advocate" (1969-70) 12 Crim. L.Q. 376 at 386-87.

24. See guidelines laid down in *R.* v. *Turner* (1970), 2 All E.R. 281 at 285 (C.A.); panel discussion in Law Soc. U.C. Special Lectures (1969) at pp. 299-311; Ratushny, "Plea Bargaining and the Public" (1972) 20 Chitty's L.J. 238.

25. Cf. CBA 4(3); IBA A-21, A-23; ABA EC 7-38, DR 7-106(C)(5);
N.B. D-5: "Undertakings should be written and the terms should be unambiguous. Counsel when giving an undertaking accepts personal responsibility unless expressly excepted."
"It has more than once been determined by the Court that if attorneys choose to practice upon loose understandings . . . they cannot expect aid from the Court if difficulties arise in carrying them out . . . .", per Barry, J. in *Ferguson* v. *Swedish-Canadian* (1912), 41 N.B.R. 217 at 220 (N.B.C.A.).
Where solicitors wrote: "on behalf of our client . . . we undertake . . ." it was held that, in the circumstances, the solicitors were personally responsible: *Re Solicitors* (1971), 1 W.W.R. 529 (B.C.C.A.).
". . . [O]ne's word should be one's bond . . . .", Lund, 1950 Lecture to the Law Society (Law Society of Upper Canada, 1956, pp. 33-34).

26. Cf. CBA 2(1); N.B. B-3, D-4; IBA C-1; ABA EC 7-36, DR 7-106(C)(6).

27. Cf. N.B. C-8; IBA A-20; ABA EC 7-19.

28. Commentary 15 to Rule 10 of the Rules of Professional Conduct of the Law Society of Upper Canada provides as follows:
"15. The lawyer should observe the following guidelines respecting communication with witnesses giving evidence:
(a)   During examination-in-chief: it is not improper for the examining lawyer to discuss with the witness any matter that has not been covered in the examination up to that point;

(b) during examination-in-chief by another lawyer of a witness who is unsympathetic to the lawyer's cause: the lawyer not conducting the examination-in-chief may properly discuss the evidence with the witness;

(c) between completion of examination-in-chief and commencement of cross-examination of the lawyer's own witness: there ought to be no discussion of the evidence given in chief or relating to any matter introduced or touched upon during the examination-in-chief;

(d) during cross-examination by an opposing lawyer: while the witness is under cross-examination the lawyer ought not to have any conversation with the witness respecting the witness's evidence or relative to any issue in the proceeding;

(e) between completion of cross-examination and commencement of re-examination: the lawyer who is going to re-examine the witness ought not to have any discussion respecting evidence that will be dealt with on re-examination;

(f) during cross-examination by the lawyer of a witness unsympathetic to the cross-examiner's cause: the lawyer may properly discuss the witness's evidence with the witness;

(g) during cross-examination by the lawyer of a witness who is sympathetic to that lawyer's cause: any conversations ought to be restricted in the same way as communications during examination-in-chief of one's own witness;

(h) during re-examination of a witness called by an opposing lawyer: if the witness is sympathetic to the lawyer's cause there ought to be no communication relating to the evidence to be given by that witness during re-examination. The lawyer may, however, properly discuss the evidence with a witness who is adverse in interest.

If there is any question whether the lawyer's behaviour may be in violation of a rule of conduct or professional etiquette, it will often be appropriate to obtain the consent of the opposing lawyer and leave of the court before engaging in conversations that may be considered improper or a breach of etiquette."

However, "It is submitted with respect that in some respects [this commentary] may inhibit the discovery of truth and go beyond what was the practice in High Court.", per Sopinka and Polin, *The Trial of an Action*, p. 106.

In Nova Scotia the rule has long existed that it is improper for counsel to communicate with a witness called in chief during a break or adjournment until the witness's cross-examination has concluded.

29. See *J. & M. Chartrand Realty Ltd.* v. *Martin* (1981), 22 C.P.C. 186 (Ont. H.C.J.).

30. Cf. ABA EC 7-15.

CHAPTER X

THE LAWYER IN PUBLIC OFFICE

RULE

The lawyer who holds public office should, in the discharge of official duties, adhere to standards of conduct as high as those that these rules require of a lawyer engaged in the practice of law.[1]

Commentary

Guiding Principles
1. The Rule applies to the lawyer who is elected or appointed to legislative or administrative office at any level of government, regardless of whether the lawyer attained such office because of professional qualifications.[2] Because such a lawyer is in the public eye, the legal profession can more readily be brought into disrepute by failure on the lawyer's part to observe its professional standards of conduct.

Conflicts of Interest
2. The lawyer who holds public office must not allow personal or other interests to conflict with the proper discharge of official duties. The lawyer holding part-time public office must not accept any private legal business where duty to the client will or may conflict with official duties. If some unforeseen conflict arises, the lawyer should terminate the professional relationship, explaining to the client that official duties must prevail. The lawyer who holds a full-time public office will not be faced with this sort of conflict, but must nevertheless guard against allowing the lawyer's independent judgement in the discharge of official duties to be influenced by the lawyer's own interest, or by the interests of persons closely related to or associated with the lawyer, or of former or prospective clients, or of former or prospective partners or associates.[3]
3. In the context of the preceding paragraph, persons closely related to or associated with the lawyer include a spouse, child, or any relative of the lawyer (or of the lawyer's spouse) living under the same roof, a trust or estate in which the lawyer has a substantial beneficial interest or for which the lawyer acts as a trustee or in a similar capacity, and a corporation of which the lawyer is a director or in which the lawyer or some closely related

or associated person holds or controls, directly or indirectly, a significant number of shares.[4]

4.   Subject to any special rules applicable to a particular public office, the lawyer holding such office who sees the possibility of a conflict of interest should declare such interest at the earliest opportunity and take no part in any consideration, discussion or vote with respect to the matter in question.[5]

Appearances before Official Bodies

5.   When the lawyer or any of the lawyer's partners or associates is a member of an official body such as, for example, a school board, municipal council or governing body, the lawyer should not appear professionally before that body. However, subject to the rules of the official body it would not be improper for the lawyer to appear professionally before a committee of such body if such partner or associate is not a member of that committee.[6]

6.   The lawyer should not represent in the same or any related matter any persons or interests that the lawyer has been concerned with in an official capacity. Similarly, the lawyer should avoid advising upon a ruling of an official body of which the lawyer either is a member or was a member at the time the ruling was made.[7]

Disclosure of Confidential Information

7.   By way of corollary to the Rule relating to confidential information, the lawyer who has acquired confidential information by virtue of holding public office should keep such information confidential and not divulge or use it even though the lawyer has ceased to hold such office.[8] (As to the taking of employment in connection with any matter in respect of which the lawyer had substantial responsibility or confidential information, see Commentary 3 of the Rule relating to avoiding questionable conduct.)

Disciplinary Action

8.   Generally speaking, a governing body will not be concerned with the way in which a lawyer holding public office carries out official responsibilities, but conduct in office that reflects adversely upon the lawyer's integrity or professional competence may subject the lawyer to disciplinary action.[9]

NOTES

1.   Cf. CBA-COD 9; IBA E-3; ABA-MR 1.11; ABA EC 8-8, DR 8-101(A).

2.   Common examples include Senators, Members of the House of Commons, members of provincial legislatures, cabinet ministers, municipal councillors, school trustees, members and officials of boards, commissions, tribunals and departments, commissioners of inquiry, arbitrators and mediators, Crown pro-

secutors and many others. For a general discussion, see Woodman, "The Lawyer in Public Life", Pitblado Lectures (Manitoba, 1971) p. 129.

3.   Cf. generally the Rule relating to conflict of interest between lawyer and client. "When a lawyer is elected to . . . (a) public office of any kind, or holds any public employment . . . his duty as the holder of such office requires him to represent the public with undivided fidelity. His obligation as a lawyer . . . continues; . . . it is improper for him to act professionally for any person . . . [who] is actively or specially interested in the promotion or defeat of legislative or other matters proposed or pending before the public body of which he is a member or by which he is employed, or before him as the holder of a public office or employment." from Brand, *Bar Associations, Attorneys and Judges* (Chicago, 1956) p. 179.

4.   Both human and financial relationships are envisaged.

5.   For example, Premier Davis of Ontario issued "Conflict of Interest Guidelines" to provincial ministers in September 1972, requiring them "while holding office . . . [to] abstain from day-to-day participation in any . . . professional activity." Specific "conflict of interest" laws have been introduced in several Canadian jurisdictions.

6.   Cf. Ont. 13; B.C. B-9(a). The Ontario ruling related specifically to municipal councillors. Local authorities have increasingly been concerned with zoning, planning and development matters in which lawyers frequently act professionally.

7.   Cf. ABA DR 9-101(A), (B): ". . . not accept private employment in matters in which the lawyer has acted in a judicial capacity or had substantial responsibility while he was a public employee."

8.   Statutory oaths of office commonly impose obligations of "official secrecy".

9.   In *Barreau de Montreal* v. *Claude Wagner* (1968), Q.B. 235 (Que. Q.B.) it was held that the respondent, then provincial Minister of Justice, was not subject to the disciplinary jurisdiction of the Bar in respect of a public speech in which he had criticized the conduct of a judge, because he was then exercising his official or "Crown" functions. In *Gagnon* v. *Bar of Montreal* (1959), B.R. 92 (Que.) it was held that on the application for readmission to practice by a former judge his conduct while in office might properly be considered by the admissions authorities.

CHAPTER XI

FEES

RULE

The lawyer shall not
(a) stipulate for, charge or accept any fee that is not fully disclosed, fair and reasonable;
(b) appropriate any funds of the client held in trust or otherwise under the lawyer's control for or on account of fees without the express authority of the client, save as permitted by the rules of the governing body.[1]

Commentary

Factors to be Considered

1. A fair and reasonable fee will depend on and reflect such factors as:
   (a) the time and effort required and spent;
   (b) the difficulty and importance of the matter;
   (c) whether special skill or service has been required and provided;
   (d) the customary charges of other lawyers of equal standing in the locality in like matters and circumstances;
   (e) in civil cases the amount involved, or the value of the subject matter;
   (f) in criminal cases the exposure and risk to the client;
   (g) the results obtained;
   (h) tariffs or scales authorized by local law;
   (i) such special circumstances as loss of other employment, urgency and uncertainty of reward;
   (j) any relevant agreement between the lawyer and the client.

A fee will not be fair and reasonable and may subject the lawyer to disciplinary proceedings if it is one that cannot be justified in the light of all pertinent circumstances, including the factors mentioned, or is so disproportionate to the services rendered as to introduce the element of fraud or dishonesty, or undue profit.[2]

2. It is in keeping with the best traditions of the legal profession to reduce or waive a fee in cases of hardship or poverty, or where the client or

prospective client would otherwise effectively be deprived of legal advice or representation.[3]

Avoidance of Controversy

3.   Breaches of this Rule and misunderstandings about fees and financial matters bring the legal profession into disrepute and reflect adversely upon the administration of justice. The lawyer should try to avoid controversy with the client over fees and should be ready to explain the basis for charges, especially if the client is unsophisticated or uninformed about the proper basis and measurements for fees. The lawyer should give the client an early and fair estimate of fees and disbursements, pointing out any uncertainties involved, so that the client may be able to make an informed decision. When something unusual or unforeseen occurs that may substantially affect the amount of the fee, the lawyer should forestall misunderstandings or disputes by explaining this to the client.[4]

Interest on Overdue Accounts

4.   Save where permitted by law or local practice, the lawyer should not charge interest on an overdue account except by prior agreement with the client and then only at a reasonable rate.[5]

Apportionment and Division of Fees

5.   The lawyer who acts for two or more clients in the same matter is under a duty to apportion the fees and disbursements equitably among them in the absence of agreement otherwise.

6.   A fee will not be a fair one within the meaning of the Rule if it is divided with another lawyer who is not a partner or associate unless (a) the client consents, either expressly or impliedly, to the employment of the other lawyer and (b) the fee is divided in proportion to the work done and responsibility assumed.[6]

Hidden Fees

7.   The fiduciary relationship that exists between lawyer and client requires full disclosure in all financial matters between them and prohibits the lawyer from accepting any hidden fees. No fee, reward, costs, commission, interest, rebate, agency or forwarding allowance or other compensation whatsoever related to the professional employment may be taken by the lawyer from anyone other than the client without full disclosure to and consent of the client. Where the lawyer's fees are being paid by someone other than the client, such as a legal aid agency, a borrower, or a personal representative, the consent of such other person will be required. So far as disbursements are concerned, only *bona fide* and specified payments to others may be included. If the lawyer is financially interested in the person to whom the disbursements are made, such as an investigating, brokerage or copying agency, the lawyer shall expressly disclose this fact to the client.[7]

Sharing Fees with Non-lawyers

8. Any arrangement whereby the lawyer directly or indirectly shares, splits or divides fees with notaries public, law students, clerks or other non-lawyers who bring or refer business to the lawyer's office is improper and constitutes professional misconduct. It is also improper for the lawyer to give any financial or other reward to such persons for referring business.[8]

9. The lawyer shall not enter into a lease or other arrangement whereby a landlord or other person directly or indirectly shares in the fees or revenues generated by the law practice.[9]

Contingent Fees

10. Except where prohibited by the laws of the jurisdiction in which the lawyer practises, it is not improper for the lawyer to enter into an arrangement with the client for a contingent fee, provided such fee is fair and reasonable and the lawyer adheres to any rules of court or local practice relating to such an arrangement.[10]

NOTES

1. Cf. CBA-COD 10; CBA 3(8), (9); Que. 3.08.01, .02; 81; B.C. B-5; Alta. 32; N.B. E-1; IBA A-8; ABA DR 2-106.

2. The proper "factors of fairness" have been many times declared by the courts. For a compilation and discussion see, e.g., *Re Solicitors* (1972), 3 O.R. 433 (Ont. H.C.) per McBride, M. at 436-37: " . . . I have not set down these factors in any sense in order of importance. In my view most of these eight factors should be considered in every case . . . time expended is not, in most cases, the overriding factor, nor even the most important. On the other hand, there are comparatively few cases where the time factor can be completely ignored."

   As to the utility of consensual local "minimum fees tariffs", see *Re Solicitors* (1970), 1 O.R. 407 (Ont. H.C.).

   "Certainty is a desirable feature of any system of law. But there are certain types of conduct . . . which cannot be satisfactorily regulated by specific statutory enactment, but are better left to the practice of juries and other tribunals of fact. They depend finally . . . on proof of the attainment of some degree [followed by a page of illustrations, most related to 'reasonableness'].", per Lord Simon, L.C. in *Knuller Ltd.* v. *D.P.P.* (1972), 2 All E.R. 898 at 929-30 (H.L.).

3. See *TWA* v. *The King* (1948), 4 D.L.R. 833 at 837 (Ont. H.C.); and cf. CBA 3(9).

4. Cf. CBA 3(10). "The question of compensation for solicitors has long been the anxious concern of the Court, both in the interests of clients and their solicitors . . . . [M]uch legislative and judicial activity was directed to the reform and settlement of procedures for fair and reasonable fees. . . . [In Ontario] there is a procedure for determining in every case where it is invoked, that a solicitor's charges are fair and reasonable.", per Wright, J. in *Re Solicitor* (1972), 1 O.R. 694 at 697 (Ont. H.C.).

   "The object of a bill of costs is to 'secure a mode by which the items of which the total bill is made up should be clearly and distinctly shown, so as to give the client an opportunity of exercising his judgment as to whether the bill was reasonable or not'.", per Riddell, J.A. in *Millar* v. *The King* (1922), 67 D.L.R. 119 at 120 (Ont.

App. Div.).
In certain provinces local law requires that clients be expressly advised of their right to have any agreement agreeing to fees in advance judicially reviewed: see N.B. E-2; *Law Society Act* R.S.M. 1970, c. L-100, s. 49; Alberta Supreme Court Rule 616(1)(f).

5.   Cf. *Solicitors Act*, R.S.O. 1980, c. 478, s.35, re-enacted by 1983, c. 21, s. 1, amended 1984, c. 11, s. 214(5), permitting interest at the rate established for pre-judgement interest from the expiration of one month after delivery of the bill. The rate of interest "shall be shown on the bill delivered", *ibid.*, s.35(4).

6.   Cf. B.C. B-5(b) and Alta. 35 (proscribing "agency fees" in consideration of the "mere introduction" of business). Cf. also ABA DR 2-107(a). The intention is not to interfere with routine agency arrangements for such services as searches or document registration in county towns or provincial capitals, etc.

7.   See particularly the Rule and Commentary respecting conflict of interest between lawyer and client for the reasons underlying these proscriptions, and *Orkin* at pp. 154-55.
The lawyer may not profit from interest on clients' trust monies in the lawyer's hands. In some provinces payment of such interest to Law Foundations and legal aid plans is now authorized.
The general principles and fiduciary duties of the law of agency apply to the lawyer-client relationship, particularly with respect to fidelity, the obligation to account, and against "secret profits". See Fridman, *The Law of Agency* (3rd ed. 1971) at pp. 30-31, 132-39, and other standard authorities on agency. It would, for example, be improper for a lawyer without express disclosure and consent to take any commission, procuration or other fee or reward from a lender, a stockbroker, a real estate or insurance agent, a trust company, a bailiff or a collection agent in consideration of the introduction by the lawyer of business from which professional work resulted to the lawyer in which the lawyer acted for or the lawyer's fees were paid by the person whose business was so introduced.
As to disbursements: "In any case where there is liability upon the part of the solicitor and there is no dishonesty, the mere fact that the amount has not been paid ought not to prevent recovery. If there should be shown any dishonesty the case would be very different ...". per Middleton, J. in *Re Solicitor* (1920), 47 O.L.R. 522 at 525 (Ont. H.C.).

8.   Cf. Ont. 9(7).

9.   *Ibid.*

10. See Williston, "The Contingent Fee in Canada" (1968) 6 Alta. L.R. 184; Arlidge, "Contingent Fees" (1974) Ottawa L.R. 374; *Thomson* v. *Wishart* (1910), 19 Man. R. 340 (Man. C.A.); *Monteith* v. *Caladine* (1965), 47 D.L.R. (2d) 322 (B.C.C.A.); *Hogan* v. *Hello* (1969), 1 N.B.R. (2d) 306. Alberta, British Columbia, Manitoba, New Brunswick, the Northwest Territories, Nova Scotia and Quebec permit regulated "contingent fees"; the remaining Canadian jurisdictions do not.

CHAPTER XII

WITHDRAWAL

RULE

The lawyer owes a duty to the client not to withdraw services except for good cause and upon notice appropriate in the circumstances.[1]

Commentary

Guiding Principles

1.   Although the client has a right to terminate the lawyer-client relationship at will, the lawyer does not enjoy the same freedom of action. Having once accepted professional employment, the lawyer should complete the task as ably as possible unless there is justifiable cause for terminating the relationship.[2]

2.   The lawyer who withdraws from employment should act so as to minimize expense and avoid prejudice to the client, doing everything reasonably possible to facilitate the expeditious and orderly transfer of the matter to the successor lawyer.[3]

3.   Where withdrawal is required or permitted by this Rule, the lawyer must comply with all applicable rules of court as well as local rules and practice.

Obligatory Withdrawal

4.   In some circumstances, the lawyer will be under a duty to withdraw. The obvious example is following discharge by the client. Other examples are (a) if the lawyer is instructed by the client to do something inconsistent with the lawyer's duty to the court and, following explanation, the client persists in such instructions; (b) if the client is guilty of dishonourable conduct in the proceedings or is taking a position solely to harass or maliciously injure another; (c) if it becomes clear that the lawyer's continued employment will lead to a breach of these Rules such as, for example, a breach of the Rules relating to conflict of interest; or (d) if it develops that the lawyer is not competent to handle the matter. In all these situations there is a duty to inform the client that the lawyer must

withdraw.[4]

Optional Withdrawal

5.   Situations where a lawyer would be entitled to withdraw, although not under a positive duty to do so, will as a rule arise only where there has been a serious loss of confidence between lawyer and client. Such a loss of confidence goes to the very basis of the relationship. Thus, the lawyer who is deceived by the client will have justifiable cause for withdrawal. Again, the refusal of the client to accept and act upon the lawyer's advice on a significant point might indicate such a loss of confidence. At the same time, the lawyer should not use the threat of withdrawal as a device to force the client into making a hasty decision on a difficult question.[5] The lawyer may withdraw if unable to obtain instructions from the client.[6]

Non-payment of Fees

6.   Failure on the part of the client after reasonable notice to provide funds on account of disbursements or fees will justify withdrawal by the lawyer unless serious prejudice to the client would result.[7]

Notice to Client

7.   No hard and fast rules can be laid down as to what will constitute reasonable notice prior to withdrawal. Where the matter is covered by statutory provisions or rules of court, these will govern. In other situations the governing principle is that the lawyer should protect the client's interests so far as possible and should not desert the client at a critical stage of a matter or at a time when withdrawal would put the client in a position of disadvantage or peril.[8]

Duty Following Withdrawal

8.   Upon discharge or withdrawal the lawyer should:
   (a)   deliver in an orderly and expeditious manner to or to the order of the client all papers and property to which the client is entitled;
   (b)   give the client all information that may be required about the case or matter;
   (c)   account for all funds of the client on hand or previously dealt with and refund any remuneration not earned during the employment;
   (d)   promptly render an account for outstanding fees and disbursements;
   (e)   co-operate with the successor lawyer for the purposes outlined in paragraph 2.

The obligation in clause (a) to deliver papers and property is subject to the lawyer's right of lien referred to in paragraph 11. In the event of conflicting claims to such papers and property, the lawyer should make every effort to have the claimants settle the dispute.[9]

9.   Co-operation with the successor lawyer will normally include providing any memoranda of fact and law that have been prepared by the lawyer in connection with the matter, but confidential information not clearly related to the matter should not be divulged without the express consent of the client.

10.   The lawyer acting for several clients in a case or matter who ceases to act for one or more of them should co-operate with the successor lawyer or lawyers to the extent permitted by this Code, and should seek to avoid any unseemly rivalry, whether real or apparent.[10]

Lien for Unpaid Fees

11.   Where upon the discharge or withdrawal of the lawyer the question of a right of lien for unpaid fees and disbursements arises, the lawyer should have due regard to the effect of its enforcement upon the client's position. Generally speaking, the lawyer should not enforce such a lien if the result would be to prejudice materially the client's position in any uncompleted matter.[11]

Duty of Successor Lawyer

12.   Before accepting employment, the successor lawyer should be satisfied that the former lawyer approves, or has withdrawn or been discharged by the client. It is quite proper for the successor lawyer to urge the client to settle or take reasonable steps toward settling or securing any account owed to the former lawyer, especially if the latter withdrew for good cause or was capriciously discharged. But if a trial or hearing is in progress or imminent, or if the client would otherwise be prejudiced, the existence of an outstanding account should not be allowed to interfere with the successor lawyer acting for the client.[12]

Dissolution of Law Firm

13.   When a law firm is dissolved, this will usually result in the termination of the lawyer-client relationship as between a particular client and one or more of the lawyers involved. In such cases, most clients will prefer to retain the services of the lawyer whom they regarded as being in charge of their business prior to the dissolution. However, the final decision rests in each case with the client, and the lawyers who are no longer retained by the client should act in accordance with the principles here set out, and in particular commentary 2.[13]

NOTES

1.   Cf. CBA-COD 11; Que. 3.03.04, .05; B.C. G-5; IBA B-4; ABA-MR 1.16; ABA EC 2-32, DR 2-110(A), (C). For cases, see 4 Can. Abr. (2d) under "Barristers and Solicitors: Termination of Relationship", paras. 101-02 and supplements. See also *Orkin*, pp. 90-95.

2.   In appeals to the Supreme Court of Canada see Rule 14(1) of that Court, whereunder the lawyer of record in the court below may be deemed to represent the client for purposes of the appeal.

3.   Cf. ABA DR 2-110(A).
     Provincial Rules of Court provide for the giving of notice of change of solicitors and for the making of applications for leave to withdraw.
     For cases see 4 Can. Abr. (2d) under "Barristers and Solicitors: Change of Solicitors", paras. 342-58 and supplements.
     In legal aid cases provincial regulations may also require notice to the plan administrators; see, e.g., in Ontario O. Reg. 59/86 as amended, s. 62(1)(a).
     On an application under the Ontario rules for an order that the lawyer has ceased to act, the supporting material must show the particular facts warranting the lawyer's ceasing to act: *Ely* v. *Rosen* (1963), 1 O.R. 47 (Ont. H.C.).
     "I have no doubt that the learned trial Judge seriously erred in law when he purported to direct counsel for the accused that he could not withdraw from the case, notwithstanding the fact that the accused, his client, apparently wished to discharge him.", per Jessup, J.A. in *Regina* v. *Spataro* (1971), 3 O.R. 419 at 422 (Ont. C.A.).

4.   Cf. CBA 3(2) and 5(5); IBA B-7; ABA DR 2-110(B).
     ". . . this case where [N.R.] is held to have sworn affidavits of discovery which were false and where the solicitor . . . should not have allowed them to be sworn if he had done his duty which he owed to the Court . . . . The solicitor cannot simply allow the client to make whatever affidavit of documents he thinks fit nor can he escape the responsibility of careful investigation or supervision. If the client will not give him the information he is entitled to require or if he insists on swearing an affidavit which the solicitor knows to be imperfect or which he has every reason to think is imperfect, then the solicitor's proper course is to withdraw from the case.", per Lord Wright in *Myers* v. *Elman* (1940), A.C. 282 at 322 (H.L.).
     For a panel discussion chaired by Gale, C.J.O. on the rights and obligations of lawyers with respect to withdrawal in criminal cases, see Law Society of Upper Canada, *Special Lectures* (1969) at pp. 295-99.

5.   Cf. ABA DR 2-119(C).
     "No solicitor . . . need put up with abuse and accusations such as were alleged to have been made here and would be fully entitled, after them, to withdraw from the case. An accusation of fraud, in fact, would make it improper for the solicitor to continue to act for the client, since it showed that the client had lost confidence in him.", per Urquhart, J. in *Re Solicitors Act; Collison* v. *Hurst* (1946), O.W.N. 668 at 671 (Ont. H.C.).

6.   Failure to instruct counsel constitutes repudiation which counsel could accept and terminate the employment.

7.   "An attorney is ordinarily justified in withdrawing if the client fails or refuses to pay or secure the proper fees or expenses of the attorney after being reasonably requested to do so.", proposition in *Corpus Juris Secundum* approved and applied in *Johnson* v. *Toronto* (1963), 1 O.R. 626 (Ont. H.C.).

8.   "If the case is scheduled to be tried on a date which will afford the accused ample time to retain another counsel, a lawyer who has not been paid the fee agreed upon may withdraw . . . . But if he waits until the eve of the trial so that there is no time for another counsel to prepare adequately . . . it becomes too late for him to withdraw. He must continue on . . . .", from panel discussion, note 4, *supra*, at pp. 295-96; and cf. Alta. 8: "If a member accepts a retainer to represent an accused at a preliminary hearing and not at the trial . . . [he] should have a clear and unambiguous understanding with his client to that effect and . . . should advise the Court at the beginning of the inquiry . . .".

9. "... [C] ounsel should be generous in accounting for any moneys which have been received but not yet earned, bearing in mind that a great deal of the time he has spent ... may be of little value to the other counsel who is required to take over.", *ibid.*, at p. 296.

As to the proper disposition of papers, which is frequently a perplexing problem, see *Cordery on Solicitors* (6th ed.) at pp. 118-20 for a discussion of law and principles and a table of categories with supporting authorities.

10. "It is quite apparent ... that the applicant dismissed the ... solicitor without just cause .... The common law right of a solicitor to exercise a lien on documents in his possession where he has been discharged without cause by his client is well recognized, subject, however, to certain exceptions ... where third parties are involved, the Court may interfere ... always upon the basis that whereas a solicitor may assert a lien ... he should not be entitled to embarrass other parties interested.", per McGillivray, J.A. in *Re Gladstone* (1972), 2 O.R. 127 at 128 (Ont. C.A.).

11. See Morden, "A Succeeding Solicitor's Duty to Protect the Accounts of the Former Solicitor" (1971) 5 Law Soc. U.C. Gaz. 257.

12. Cf. CBA 4(1).

13. "Subject to any question of lien, the client's papers in possession of the firm belong to the client and cannot be the subject of agreement as against him, but as *between themselves* solicitors can agree that on dissolution the clients of the old firm and their papers shall either be divided between the dissolving partners, or belong to those continuing the business of the firm ....", *Cordery on Solicitors* (6th ed.) at pp. 463-64 (emphasis added).

CHAPTER XIII

THE LAWYER AND THE ADMINISTRATION OF JUSTICE

RULE

The lawyer should encourage public respect for and try to improve the administration of justice.[1]

Commentary

Guiding Principles

1.   The admission to and continuance in the practice of law imply a basic commitment by the lawyer to the concept of equal justice for all within an open, ordered and impartial system. However, judicial institutions will not function effectively unless they command the respect of the public. Because of changes in human affairs and the imperfection of human institutions, constant efforts must be made to improve the administration of justice and thereby maintain public respect for it.[2]

2.   The lawyer, by training, opportunity and experience, is in a position to observe the workings and discover the strengths and weaknesses of laws, legal institutions and public authorities. The lawyer should, therefore, lead in seeking improvements in the legal system, but any criticisms and proposals should be *bona fide* and reasoned.[3]

Scope of the Rule

3.   The obligation outlined in the Rule is not restricted to the lawyer's professional activities but is a general responsibility resulting from the lawyer's position in the community. The lawyer's responsibilities are greater than those of a private citizen. The lawyer must not subvert the law by counselling or assisting in activities that are in defiance of it and must do nothing to lessen the respect and confidence of the public in the legal system of which the lawyer is a part. The lawyer should take care not to weaken or destroy public confidence in legal institutions or authorities by broad irresponsible allegations of corruption or partiality. The lawyer in public life must be particularly careful in this regard because the mere fact of being a lawyer will lend weight and credibility to any public statements.[4]

For the same reason, the lawyer should not hesitate to speak out against an injustice. (As to test cases, see commentary 8 of the Rule relating to advising clients.)

Criticism of the Tribunal

4.   Although proceedings and decisions of tribunals are properly subject to scrutiny and criticism by all members of the public, including lawyers, members of tribunals are often prohibited by law or custom from defending themselves. Their inability to do so imposes special responsibilities upon lawyers. Firstly, the lawyer should avoid criticism that is petty, intemperate or unsupported by a *bona fide* belief in its real merit, bearing in mind that in the eyes of the public, professional knowledge lends weight to the lawyer's judgements or criticism. Secondly, if the lawyer has been involved in the proceedings, there is the risk that any criticism may be, or may appear to be, partisan rather than objective. Thirdly, where a tribunal is the object of unjust criticism, the lawyer, as a participant in the administration of justice, is uniquely able to and should support the tribunal, both because its members cannot defend themselves and because the lawyer is thereby contributing to greater public understanding of and therefore respect for the legal system.[5]

Improving the Administration of Justice

5.   The lawyer who seeks legislative or administrative changes should disclose whose interest is being advanced, whether it be the lawyer's interest, that of a client, or the public interest. The lawyer may advocate such changes on behalf of a client without personally agreeing with them, but the lawyer who purports to act in the public interest should espouse only those changes that the lawyer conscientiously believes to be in the public interest.[6]

NOTES

1.   Cf. CBA-COD 12. IBA, "Duty to the Court": "In view of the vital part played by lawyers in the administration of justice, they are under an obligation to strive to maintain respect for that administration . . .".

2.   Cf. the traditional barristers' oath: ". . . to protect and defend the right and interest of such of your fellow-citizens as may employ you . . . . You shall not pervert the law to favour or prejudice any man . . .".
      ABA ECs 8-1, 8-2 and 8-9: "Changes in human affairs and imperfections in human institutions make necessary constant efforts to maintain and improve our legal system. This system should function in a manner that commands public respect and fosters the use of legal remedies to achieve redress of grievances . . . . Rules of law are deficient if they are not just, understandable and responsive to the needs of society . . . . The advancement of our legal system is of vital importance in maintaining the rule of law and in facilitating orderly changes . . .".

3.   ABA ECs 8-1, 8-2: "By reason of education and experience, lawyers are especially qualified to recognize deficiencies in the legal system and to initiate corrective

measures therein . . . . [The lawyer] should encourage the simplification of laws and the repeal or amendment of laws that are outmoded. Likewise, legal procedures should be improved whenever experience indicates a change is needed."

4.   Cf. CBA Preamble: "The lawyer is more than a mere citizen . . .". "[L]awyers, because of *what* they are as opposed to *who* they are . . . are required to assume responsibilities of citizenship well beyond [the basic requirements of good citizenship] . . . This . . . is necessary because we are the profession to which society has entrusted the administration of law and the dispensing of justice.", MacKimmie, "Presidential Address" (1963) 6 Can. B.J. 347 at 348. For lucid and divergent views as to the limits to which lawyers may properly go in "defying the law" see editorial "Civil Disobedience and the Lawyer" (1967) 1(3) Law Soc. U.C. Gaz. 5 and response thereto in (1968) 2 Law Soc. U.C. Gaz. 44.

5.   Cf. CBA 2(2) and ABA EC 8-6. Tribunals generally possess summary "contempt" powers, but these are circumscribed and are not lightly resorted to. Means exist through Attorneys-General and Judicial Councils for the investigation and remedying of specific complaints of official misbehaviour and neglect; in particular cases these should be resorted to in preference to public forums and the media.

6.   Cf. ABA EC 8-4.

CHAPTER XIV

ADVERTISING, SOLICITATION AND MAKING LEGAL SERVICES AVAILABLE

RULE

Lawyers should make legal services available to the public in an efficient and convenient manner that will command respect and confidence, and by means that are compatible with the integrity, independence and effectiveness of the profession.[1]

Commentary

Guiding Principles

1.   It is essential that a person requiring legal services be able to find a qualified lawyer with a minimum of difficulty or delay. In a relatively small community where lawyers are well known, the person will usually be able to make an informed choice and select a qualified lawyer in whom to have confidence. However, in larger centres these conditions will often not obtain. As the practice of law becomes increasingly complex and many individual lawyers restrict their activities to particular fields of law, the reputations of lawyers and their competence or qualification in particular fields may not be sufficiently well known to enable a person to make an informed choice. Thus one who has had little or no contact with lawyers or who is a stranger in the community may have difficulty finding a lawyer with the special skill required for a particular task. Telephone directories, legal directories and referral services may help find a lawyer, but not necessarily the right one for the work involved.[2] Advertising of legal services by the lawyer may assist members of the public and thereby result in increased access to the legal system. Where local rules permit, the lawyer may, therefore, advertise legal services to the general public.

2.   When considering whether advertising in a particular area meets the public need, consideration must be given to the clientele to be served. For example, in a small community with a stable population a person requiring a lawyer for a particular purpose will not have the same difficulty in selecting one as someone in a newly-established community or a large city. Thus the governing body must have freedom of action in determining the

nature and content of advertising that will best meet the community need.[3]

3.   Despite the lawyer's economic interest in earning a living, advertising, direct solicitation or any other means by which the lawyer seeks to make legal services more readily available to the public must comply with any rules prescribed by the governing body, must be consistent with the public interest and must not detract from the integrity, independence or effectiveness of the legal profession. They must not mislead the uninformed or arouse unattainable hopes and expectations, because this could result in distrust of legal institutions and lawyers. They must not adversely affect the quality of legal services, nor must they be so undignified, in bad taste or otherwise offensive as to be prejudicial to the interests of the public or the legal profession.

Finding a Lawyer

4.   The lawyer who is consulted by a prospective client should be ready to assist in finding the right lawyer to deal with the problem. If unable to act, for example because of lack of qualification in the particular field, the lawyer should assist in finding a practitioner who is qualified and able to act. Such assistance should be given willingly and, except in very special circumstances, without charge.[4]

5.   The lawyer may also assist in making legal services available by participating in legal aid plans and referral services, by engaging in programs of public information, education or advice concerning legal matters, and by being considerate of those who seek advice but are inexperienced in legal matters or cannot readily explain their problems.

6.   The lawyer has a general right to decline particular employment (except when assigned as counsel by a court) but it is a right the lawyer should be slow to exercise if the probable result would be to make it very difficult for a person to obtain legal advice or representation. Generally speaking, the lawyer should not exercise the right merely because the person seeking legal services or that person's cause is unpopular or notorious, or because powerful interests or allegations of misconduct or malfeasance are involved, or because of the lawyer's private opinion about the guilt of the accused. As stated in commentary 4, the lawyer who declines employment should assist the person to obtain the services of another lawyer competent in the particular field and able to act.[5]

Enforcement of Restrictive Rules

7.   The lawyer should adhere to rules made by the governing body with respect to making legal services available and respecting advertising, but rigid adherence to restrictive rules should be enforced with discretion where the lawyer who may have infringed such rules acted in good faith in trying to make legal services available more efficiently, economically and conveniently than they would otherwise have been.

NOTES

1. Cf. CBA-COD 13; ABA-MR 7; ABA Canon 2, EC 2-1; IBA at p. 30.

2. Cf. ABA ECs 2-6, 2-7.

3. At present the governing bodies and professional conduct committees, through rulings, by-laws, rules and opinions, regulate the details of permissible and impermissible advertising within their jurisdictions. Such matters as signs, name-plates, professional cards, announcements, letterheads, listings, firm names and "specialist" representations are dealt with. The regulations vary considerably from place to place and change from time to time. No attempt is here made to collect or epitomize them. For summaries of rulings and of illustrative decisions in these areas see *Orkin* at pp. 177-88, *Cordery on Solicitors* (6th ed.) at pp. 486-87.

4. Cf. ABA EC 2-8.

5. Cf. N.B. C-4; ABA ECs 2-26 to 2-29; *Orkin* at pp. 87-88.

CHAPTER XV

RESPONSIBILITY TO THE PROFESSION GENERALLY

RULE

The lawyer should assist in maintaining the integrity of the profession and should participate in its activities.[1]

Commentary

Guiding Principles

1. Unless the lawyer who tends to depart from proper professional conduct is checked at an early stage, loss or damage to clients or others may ensue. Evidence of minor breaches may, on investigation, disclose a more serious situation or may indicate the beginning of a course of conduct that would lead to serious breaches in the future. It is, therefore, proper (unless it be privileged or otherwise unlawful) for a lawyer to report to a governing body any occurrences involving a breach of this Code. Where, however, there is a reasonable likelihood that someone will suffer serious damage as a consequence of an apparent breach, for example where a shortage of trust funds is involved, the lawyer has an obligation to the profession to report the matter unless it is privileged or otherwise unlawful to do so. In all cases, the report must be made *bona fide* without malice or ulterior motive.[2] Further, subject to local rules, the lawyer must not act on a client's instructions to recover from another lawyer funds allegedly misappropriated by that other lawyer unless the client authorizes disclosure to the governing body and the lawyer makes such disclosure.

2. The lawyer has a duty to reply promptly to any communication from the governing body.[3]

3. The lawyer should not in the course of a professional practice write letters, whether to a client, another lawyer or any other person, that are abusive, offensive or otherwise totally inconsistent with the proper tone of a professional communication from a lawyer.[4]

Participation in Professional Activities

4. In order that the profession may discharge its public responsibility of

providing independent and competent legal services, the individual lawyer should do everything possible to assist the profession to function properly and effectively. In this regard, participation in such activities as law reform, continuing legal education, tutorials, legal aid programs, community legal services, professional conduct and discipline, liaison with other professions and other activities of the governing body or local, provincial or national associations, although often time-consuming and without tangible reward, is essential to the maintenance of a strong, independent and useful profession.[5]

NOTES

1. Cf. CBA-COD 14; CBA 5(1); ABA-MR 8; ABA Canon 1.
    "The legal profession . . . has emerged over the centuries in order to fill a pressing public need for protection . . . under the law of the rights and liberties of the individual, however humble, if necessary against the state itself.", IBA introductory.
    "Public confidence in the profession would be shaken if such conduct were tolerated . . . no solicitor could escape [striking off] simply by showing that there had been no dishonesty and no concealment, and that no client had suffered . . .", per Parker, L.C.J. in *re a Solicitor* (1959), 193 Sol. Jour. 875 (Q.B.D.).

2. Cf. CBA 5(1); Ont. 13; B.C. F-3; ABA DR 1-103, EC 1-4. Alta. 22: "It is conduct unbecoming . . . not to [report instances] when they clearly involve a shortage of trust funds or a breach of an undertaking."

3. Cf. Ont. 13(3); Alta. 18; N.B. D-1; Sask. 12. "The reprehensible thing about the solicitor's conduct is his indefensible ignoring of the communications of the Law Society . . .", per Walsh, J. in *In re X., a Solicitor* (1920), 16 Alta. L.R. 542 at 543.

4. Cf. IBA D-6.

5. Cf. ABA ECs 1-4, 2-25, 6-2, 8-1, 8-2, 8-3, 8-9, 9-6.

CHAPTER XVI

RESPONSIBILITY TO LAWYERS INDIVIDUALLY

RULE

The lawyer's conduct toward other lawyers should be characterized by courtesy and good faith.[1]

Commentary

Guiding Principles

1. Public interest demands that matters entrusted to the lawyer be dealt with effectively and expeditiously. Fair and courteous dealing on the part of each lawyer engaged in a matter will contribute materially to this end. The lawyer who behaves otherwise does a disservice to the client, and neglect of the Rule will impair the ability of lawyers to perform their function properly.[2]

2. Any ill feeling that may exist or be engendered between clients, particularly during litigation, should never be allowed to influence lawyers in their conduct and demeanour toward each other or the parties. The presence of personal animosity between lawyers involved in a matter may cause their judgement to be clouded by emotional factors and hinder the proper resolution of the matter. Personal remarks or references between them should be avoided. Haranguing or offensive tactics interfere with the orderly administration of justice and have no place in our legal system.[3]

3. The lawyer should accede to reasonable requests for trial dates, adjournments, waivers of procedural formalities and similar matters that do not prejudice the rights of the client. The lawyer who knows that another lawyer has been consulted in a matter should not proceed by default in the matter without enquiry and warning.[4]

Avoidance of Sharp Practices

4. The lawyer should avoid sharp practice and not take advantage of or act without fair warning upon slips, irregularities or mistakes on the part of other lawyers not going to the merits or involving any sacrifice of the

client's rights. The lawyer should not, unless required by the transaction, impose on other lawyers impossible, impractical or manifestly unfair conditions of trust, including those with respect to time restraints and the payment of penalty interest.

5.   The lawyer should not use a tape-recorder or other device to record a conversation, whether with a client, another lawyer or anyone else, even if lawful, without first informing the other person of the intention to do so.[5]

6.   The lawyer should answer with reasonable promptness all professional letters and communications from other lawyers that require an answer and should be punctual in fulfilling all commitments.[6]

Undertakings

7.   The lawyer should give no undertaking that cannot be fulfilled, should fulfill every undertaking given, and should scrupulously honour any trust condition once accepted. Undertakings and trust conditions should be written or confirmed in writing and should be absolutely unambiguous in their terms. If the lawyer giving an undertaking does not intend to accept personal responsibility, this should be stated clearly in the undertaking itself. In the absence of such a statement, the person to whom the undertaking is given is entitled to expect that the lawyer giving it will honour it personally.[7] If the lawyer is unable or unwilling to honour a trust condition imposed by someone else, the subject of the trust condition should be immediately returned to the person imposing the trust condition unless its terms can be forthwith amended in writing on a mutually agreeable basis.

8.   The lawyer should not communicate upon or attempt to negotiate or compromise a matter directly with any party who is represented by a lawyer except through or with the consent of that lawyer.[8]

Acting Against Another Lawyer

9.   The lawyer should avoid ill-considered or uninformed criticism of the competence, conduct, advice or charges of other lawyers, but should be prepared, when requested, to advise and represent a client in a complaint involving another lawyer.[9]

10.   The same courtesy and good faith should characterize the lawyer's conduct toward lay persons lawfully representing others or themselves.

11.   The lawyer who is retained by another lawyer as counsel or adviser in a particular matter should act only as counsel or adviser and respect the relationship between the other lawyer and the client.

NOTES

1.   Cf. CBA-COD 167; CBA 4(1), (2), (4); Ont. 14; ABA ECs 7-37 and 7-38, DR 7-101(A)(1).

2. "...besides the duty which an attorney owes to the court and his client, he is bound as regards the opposite party and his professional brethren, to conduct his business with fairness and propriety.", *Dobie* v. *McFarlane* (1832), 2 U.C.Q.B. (O.S.) 285 at 323. See also N.B. D-4.

3. Cf. CBA 4(2); *Orkin* at pp. 131-32. N.B. D-4: "... it is the duty of counsel to 'try the merits of the cause and not to try each other'."

4. Cf. CBA 4(2); ABA ECs 7-38 and 7-39. "... the attorney, I think, is not bound to lay before his client every opportunity he may have of shutting out the other party from a hearing, nor bound to take or follow the direction of his client as to the degree of liberality which he shall observe in his practice.", per Robinson, C.J. in *Shaw et al.* v. *Nickerson* (1850), 7 U.C.Q.B. 541 at 544.

5. Cf. CBA 4(4), "Truth and not trickery, simplicity and not duplicity, candour and not craftiness in the conduct of legal affairs...", per Chancellor Boyd in "Address on Legal Ethics" (1905) 4 Can. L. Rev. 85. ABA EC 7-38: "He should follow local customs of courtesy or practice, unless he gives timely notice to opposing counsel of his intention not to do so." The lawyer who intends to insist on "Peremptory Rules" should make this clear.
    "... [T]o build up a client's case on the slips of an opponent is not the duty of a professional man ... Solicitors do not do their duty to their clients by insisting upon the strict letter of their rights. That is the sort of thing which, if permitted, brings the administration of justice into odium.", per Middleton, J. in *Re Arthur and Town of Meaford* (1915), 34 O.L.R. 231 at 233-34 (Ont. H.C.).
    "... [W]e do not think that [the defendant's attorney's] conduct was marked with candor in not drawing the plaintiff's attorneys' notice to such objections in the procedure as he had or intended to insist upon until the day before the opening of the court at which the trial was to be had...", per Gwynne, J. in *Cushman et al.* v. *Reid* (1869), 20 U.C.C.P. 147 at 153-54.
    As to tape recordings, see (1972) 6 Law Soc. U.C. Gaz. 15.

6. Alta. 20: "Failure to reply to letters or other communications from another member is at the very least discourteous... this practice frequently places the other member in an awkward and embarrassing position ... and tends to lower the reputation of the whole profession."

7. Cf. paragraph 11 of the Rule relating to the lawyer as advocate; Ont. 14(6); Alta. 17: "... [T]he use of such words as 'on behalf of my client' or 'on behalf of the vendor' does not relieve the solicitor giving the undertaking of personal responsibility." B.C. D-2: "... [D]ifficulties may arise if [members] give undertakings on behalf of clients since clients may change instructions or solicitors. An undertaking given by one solicitor to another can be released or altered only by the latter and not by his client. The giving of an uncertified cheque is an undertaking, except in the most unusual and unforeseen circumstances the justification for which rests upon the member, that such cheque will be paid...".

8. Cf. CBA 4(3); B.C. D-1(a); Alta. 16; N.B. D-3; ABA EC 7-18; *Nelson* v. *Murphy et al.* (1957), 9 D.L.R. (2d) 195 (Man. C.A.) per Tritschler, J.A. at p. 213: "The principle was laid down long ago... that once it appears a person has an attorney there can be no effective dealing except through him ... a lawyer 'should never in any way... attempt to negotiate or compromise the matter directly with any party represented by a lawyer except *through* such lawyer'."
    "... [The lawyer should] not hold any communication of the kind that passed here, except with the solicitor of the opposite party, and even had the defendants come to the office of then plaintiff's solicitor, as the latter alleges, of his own accord, he should have refused to negotiate with him personally", per Van Koughnet, C. in *Bank of Montreal* v. *Wilson* (1867), 2 Chy. Chs. 117 and 119 (U.C. Chy. Chs. 117 and 119 (U.C. Chy.).

9.   Cf. CBA 5(1); IBA C-4; ABA EC 2-28; *Orkin* at pp. 97-98. See also paragraph 9 of the Rule relating to making legal services available.

CHAPTER XVII

PRACTICE BY UNAUTHORIZED PERSONS

RULE

The lawyer should assist in preventing the unauthorized practice of law.[1]

Commentary

Guiding Principles

1. Statutory provisions against the practice of law by unauthorized persons are for the protection of the public. Unauthorized persons may have technical or personal ability, but they are immune from control, regulation and, in the case of misconduct, from discipline by any governing body. Their competence and integrity have not been vouched for by an independent body representative of the legal profession. Morever, the client of a lawyer who is authorized to practise has the protection and benefit of the lawyer-client privilege, the lawyer's duty of secrecy, the professional standards of care that the law requires of lawyers, as well as the authority that the courts exercise over them. Other safeguards include group professional liability insurance, rights with respect to the taxation of bills, rules respecting trust monies, and requirements for the maintenance of compensation funds.[2]

Suspended or Disbarred Persons

2. The lawyer should not, without the approval of the governing body, employ in any capacity having to do with the practice of law (a) a lawyer who is under suspension as a result of disciplinary proceedings, or (b) a person who has been disbarred as a lawyer or has been permitted to resign while facing disciplinary proceedings and has not been reinstated.[3]

Supervision of Employees

3. The lawyer must assume complete professional responsibility for all business entrusted to the lawyer, maintaining direct supervision over staff and assistants such as students, clerks and legal assistants to whom particular tasks and functions may be delegated. The lawyer who practises

alone or operates a branch or part-time office should ensure that all matters requiring a lawyer's professional skill and judgement are dealt with by a lawyer qualified to do the work and that legal advice is not given by unauthorized persons, whether in the lawyer's name or otherwise. Furthermore, the lawyer should approve the amount of any fee to be charged to a client.[4]

Legal Assistants

4.   There are many tasks that can be performed by a legal assistant working under the supervision of a lawyer. It is in the interests of the profession and the public for the delivery of more efficient, comprehensive and better quality legal services that the training and employment of legal assistants be encouraged.

5.   Subject to general and specific restrictions that may be established by local rules and practice, a legal assistant may perform any task delegated and supervised by a lawyer so long as the lawyer maintains a direct relationship with the client and assumes full professional responsibility for the work. Legal assistants shall not perform any of the duties that lawyers only may perform or do things that lawyers themselves may not do. Generally speaking, the question of what the lawyer may delegate to a legal assistant turns on the distinction between the special knowledge of the legal assistant and the professional legal judgement of the lawyer, which must be exercised whenever it is required.

6.   A legal assistant should be permitted to act only under the supervision of a lawyer. Adequacy of supervision will depend on the type of legal matter, including the degree of standardization and repetitiveness of the matter as well as the experience of the legal assistant, both generally and with regard to the particular matter. The burden rests on the lawyer who employs a legal assistant to educate the latter about the duties to which the legal assistant may be assigned and also to supervise on a continuing basis the way in which the legal assistant carries them out so that the work of the legal assistant will be shaped by the lawyer's judgement.

NOTES

1.   Cf. CBA-COD 15; CBA 5(1), (2); IBA E-5 and E-6; ABA-MR 5.5; ABA Canon 3, DRs 3-101 (A), (B) and 3-103(2).

2.   Cases and statutes provide that certain acts amount to "the practice of law"; see, for example:
B.C.: *Barristers and Solicitors Act*, R.S.B.C. 1979, c. 26, ss. 1, 80.
Man.: *Law Society Act*, R.S.M. 1970, c. L-100, s. 48(1), (2).
N.B.: *Barristers Society Act*, S.N.B. 1931, c. 50, s. 14A as amended by S.N.B. 1937, c. 30.
Nfld.: *Law Society Act*, R.S.N. 1970, c. 201, s. 76(2).
N.S.: *Barristers and Solicitors Act*, R.S.N.S. c. B-2, s. 4(2).
P.E.I.: *Law Society and Legal Profession Act*, R.S.P.E.I. 1974, c. L-9, s. 21.

Que.: *Bar Act*, R.S.Q. 1977, c. B-1, s. 128.
The statutes of all provinces prohibit the practice of law by unauthorized persons:
Alta.: *Legal Profession Act*, R.S.A. c. L-9, s. 93.
B.C.: *supra*, s. 77.
Man.: *supra*, s. 48(1).
N.B.: *supra*, s. 14(3).
Nfld.: *supra*, s. 76(1).
N.S.: *supra*, s. 4(1).
Ont.: *Law Society Act*, R.S.O. 1980, c. 233, s. 50(1), (2).
P.E.I.: *supra*, s. 19.
Que.: *supra*, ss. 132 et seq.
Sask.: *Legal Profession Act*, R.S.S. c. L-10, s. 5.
"To protect the public against persons who . . . set themselves up as competent to perform services that imperatively require the training and learning of a solicitor, although such persons are without either learning or experience to qualify them, is an urgent public service.", per Robertson, C.J.O. in *Rex ex rel. Smith* v. *Ott* (1950) O.R. 493 at 496 (Ont. C.A.)
"When a man says in effect, I am not a lawyer but I will do the work of a lawyer for you he is offering his services as a lawyer. In offering his services as a lawyer he is holding himself out as a lawyer even though he makes it clear he is not a properly qualified lawyer.", per Miller, C.C.J. in *Regina* v. *Woods* (1962), O.W.N. 27 at 30.
See, generally, *Orkin* at pp. 350-53, *Bennion* at p. 54.

3. Cf. Ont. 19, 20; B.C. F-4. In cases of hardship or illness and for other good cause governing bodies may well permit regulated and limited employment, for example to help rehabilitate an offender or one recovering from a disability. Their concern is to protect the public, not necessarily to inhibit individuals.

4. Cf. B.C. G-2; Alta. 40; IBA E-4 and E-6; ABA ECs 3-5 and 3-6. See also "Delegation of Authority by Solicitors" (1968) 3 Law Soc. U.C. Gaz. 23.

CHAPTER XVIII

PUBLIC APPEARANCES AND PUBLIC STATEMENTS BY LAWYERS

RULE

The lawyer who engages in public appearances and public statements should do so in conformity with the principles of the Code.

Commentary

Guiding Principles

1.   The lawyer who makes public appearances and public statements should behave in the same way as when dealing with clients, fellow practitioners and the courts. Dealings with the media are simply an extension of the lawyer's conduct in a professional capacity. The fact that an appearance is outside a courtroom or law office does not excuse conduct that would be considered improper in those contexts.

Public Statements Concerning Clients

2.   The lawyer's duty to the client demands that before making a public statement concerning the client's affairs, the lawyer must first be satisfied that any communication is in the best interests of the client and within the scope of the retainer. The lawyer owes a duty to the client to be qualified to represent the client effectively before the public and not to permit any personal interest or other cause to conflict with the client's interests.

3.   When acting as an advocate, the lawyer should refrain from expressing personal opinions about the merits of the client's case.

Standard of Conduct

4.   The lawyer should, where possible, encourage public respect for and try to improve the administration of justice. In particular, the lawyer should treat fellow practitioners, the courts and tribunals with respect, integrity and courtesy. Lawyers are subject to a separate and higher standard of conduct than that which might incur the sanction of the court.

5.   The lawyer who makes public appearances and public statements

must comply with the requirements of commentary 3 of the Rule relating to advertising, solicitation and making legal services available.

Contacts with the Media

6.   The media have recently shown greater interest in legal matters than they did formerly. This is reflected in more coverage of the passage of legislation at national and provincial levels, as well as of cases before the courts that may have social, economic or political significance. This interest has been heightened by the enactment of the *Canadian Charter of Rights and Freedoms*. As a result, media reporters regularly seek out the views not only of lawyers directly involved in particular court proceedings but also of lawyers who represent special interest groups or have recognized expertise in a given field in order to obtain information or provide commentary.

7.   Where the lawyer, by reason of professional involvement or otherwise, is able to assist the media in conveying accurate information to the public, it is proper for the lawyer to do so, provided that there is no infringement of the lawyer's obligations to the client, the profession, the courts or the administration of justice, and provided also that the lawyer's comments are made *bona fide* and without malice or ulterior motive.

8.   The lawyer may make contact with the media in a non-legal setting to publicize such things as fund-raising, expansion of hospitals or universities, promoting public instiitutions or political organizations, or speaking on behalf of organizations that represent various racial, religious or other special interest groups. This is a well-established and completely proper role for the lawyer to play in view of the obvious contribution it makes to the community.

9.   The lawyer is often called upon to comment publicly on the effectiveness of existing statutory or legal remedies, on the effect of particular legislation or decided cases, or to offer an opinion on causes that have been or are about to be instituted. It is permissible to do this in order to assist the public to understand the legal issues involved.

10.   The lawyer may also be involved as an advocate for special interest groups whose objective is to bring about changes in legislation, government policy or even a heightened public awareness about certain issues, and the lawyer may properly comment publicly about such changes.

11.   Given the variety of cases that can arise in the legal system, whether in civil, criminal or administrative matters, it is not feasible to set down guidelines that would anticipate every possible situation. In some circumstances, the lawyer should have no contact at all with the media; in others, there may be a positive duty to contact the media in order to serve the client properly. The latter situation will arise more often when dealing with administrative boards and tribunals that are instruments of government policy and hence susceptible to public opinion.

12.   The lawyer should bear in mind when making a public appearance or giving a statement that ordinarily the lawyer will have no control over any editing that may follow, or the context in which the appearance or statement may be used.

13.   This Rule should not be construed in such a way as to discourage constructive comment or criticism.

CHAPTER XIX

AVOIDING QUESTIONABLE CONDUCT

RULE

The lawyer should observe the rules of professional conduct set out in the Code in the spirit as well as in the letter.[1]

Commentary

Guiding Principles

1.   Public confidence in the administration of justice and the legal profession may be eroded by irresponsible conduct on the part of the individual lawyer. For that reason, even the appearance of impropriety should be avoided.[2]

2.   Our justice system is designed to try issues in an impartial manner and decide them upon the merits. Statements or suggestions that the lawyer could or would try to circumvent the system should be avoided because they might bring the lawyer, the legal profession and the administration of justice into disrepute.[3]

Duty after Leaving Public Employment

3.   After leaving public employment, the lawyer should not accept employment in connection with any matter in which the lawyer had substantial responsibility or confidential information prior to leaving, because to do so would give the appearance of impropriety even if none existed. However, it would not be improper for the lawyer to act professionally in such a matter on behalf of the particular public body or authority by which the lawyer had formerly been employed.[4] As to confidential government information acquired when the lawyer was a public officer or employee, see commentary 14 of the Rule relating to confidential information.

Retired Judges

4.   A judge who returns to practice after retiring or resigning from the bench should not (without the approval of the governing body) appear as a lawyer before the court of which the former judge was a member or before

courts of inferior jurisdiction thereto in the province where the judge exercised judicial functions. If in a given case the former judge should be in a preferred position by reason of having held judicial office, the administration of justice would suffer; if the reverse were true, the client might suffer. There may, however, be cases where a governing body would consider that no preference or appearance of preference would result, for example, where the judge resigned for good reason after only a very short time on the bench. In this paragraph "judge" refers to one who was apppointed as such under provincial legislation or section 96 of the *Constitution Act, 1982* and "courts" include chambers and administrative boards and tribunals.[5]

5.   Conversely, although it may be unavoidable in some circumstances or areas, generally speaking the lawyer should not appear before a judge if by reason of relationship or past association, the lawyer would appear to be in a preferred position.[6]

Inserting Retainer in Client's Will

6.   Without express instructions from the client, it is improper for the lawyer to insert in the client's will a clause directing the executor to retain the lawyer's services in the administration of the estate.[7]

Duty to Meet Financial Obligations

7.   The lawyer has a professional duty, quite apart from any legal liability, to meet financial obligations incurred or assumed in the course of practice when called upon to do so. Examples are agency accounts, obligations to members of the profession, fees or charges of witnesses, sheriffs, special examiners, registrars, reporters and public officials as well as the deductible under a governing body's errors and omissions insurance policy.[8]

Dealings with Unrepresented Persons

8.   The lawyer should not undertake to advise an unrepresented person, but should urge such a person to obtain independent legal advice and, if the unrepresented person does not do so, the lawyer must take care to see that such person is not proceeding under the impression that the lawyer is protecting such person's interests. If the unrepresented person requests the lawyer to advise or act in the matter, the lawyer should be governed by the considerations outlined in the Rule relating to impartiality and conflict of interest between clients.[9] The lawyer may have an obligation to a person whom the lawyer does not represent, whether or not such person is represented by a lawyer.

Bail

9.   The lawyer shall not stand bail for an accused person for whom the lawyer or a partner or associate is acting, except where there is a family

relationship with the accused in which case the person should not be represented by the lawyer but may be represented by a partner or associate.

Standard of Conduct

10.   The lawyer should try at all times to observe a standard of conduct that reflects credit on the legal profession and the administration of justice generally and inspires the confidence, respect and trust of both clients and the community.

NOTES

1.   Cf. CBA-COD 17; CBA 5(6): "... [T]he oath of office ... is not a mere form, but is a solemn undertaking." ABA Canon 9: "A lawyer should avoid even the appearance of professional impropriety."
Cf. dictum of Hewart, L.C.J. in *The King* v. *Sussex Justices* (1924), 1 K.B. 256 at 259 (K.B.D.): "... [It] is of fundamental importance that justice should not only be done, but should manifestly and undoubtedly be seen to be done."

2.   Cf. ABA EC 9-1. In *Re Novak and Law Society* (1973) 31 D.L.R. (3d) 89 (B.C.S.C.) (sustaining the disbarment of a lawyer who had negotiated a reward through the police for the return of stolen securities) the Discipline Committee said (at p. 95): "In exposing himself to these situations the Respondent divested himself of the dignity and forthright dealing that one may expect of a lawyer, gave rise to the reasonable conclusion that he was associated with the possessors of the goods, and that he was participating in some way in the reward .... Whether in fact he was doing so is perhaps not important."

3.   Cf. ABA EC 9-4: "There should be the very contrary to the secrecy and subterfuge which marks every step of this transaction, dishonourable alike to counsel and the magistrate.", per Baxter, C.J. in *The King* v. *LeBlanc and Long* (1938-39) 13 M.P.R. 343 at 357 (N.B. App. Div.).

4.   Cf. ABA DR 9-101(B).

5.   Cf. Ont. 15: "... [I]f a man should step down [from the Bench] and ... perhaps challenge the decisions which he pronounced, or even fail to support them in argument, he will shake the authority of the judicial limb of government, and mar the prestige and dignity of the Courts of Justice ...", per Kennedy, C.J. in *Re Solicitors Act and O'Connor* (1930) I.R. 623 at 631 (Irish H.C.).

6.   Cf. paragraph 1(c) of the Rule relating to the lawyer as advocate; *Orkin* at p. 43.

7.   Cf. Alta. 28. Such a direction does not bind the executor: *Re Croft* (1960) O.W.N. 171 (Ont. H.C.).

8.   Art. 19 of the International Code of Ethics provides: "A lawyer who engages a foreign colleague to advise on a case or to cooperate in handling it, is responsible for the payment of the latter's charges except express agreement to the contrary. When a lawyer directs a client to a foreign colleague he is not responsible ...". Cf. also IBA D-10.

9.   Cf. *Orkin* at pp. 127-28.
"In every case where there is the least doubt ... as to whether the other party is capable of protecting himself, it is the duty of [the] solicitor ... to see, if possible, that the other party is adequately represented; and, in the absence of such independent representation, it is the duty of the Court to scrutinize ... to see whether ... there has been any overreaching or unconscionable dealing.", per

Orde, J. in *Chait & Leon* v. *Harding* (1920-21) 19 O.W.N. 20 at 21 (Ont. H.C.). "It was [the solicitor's] duty to see that the infirm person was adequately protected or had independent advice. If [he] regarded himself as the adviser of the aged plaintiff, he should have insisted that proper arrangements protecting [him] were entered into . . .", per Middleton, J. in *Finney* v. *Tripp* (1922) 22 O.W.N. 429 at 430 (Ont. H.C.).

ABBREVIATIONS

Short-form references to Canons, Codes, Rulings and particular writings are as follows:

Alta	Rulings of the Benchers of the Law Society of Alberta, contained in the *Professional Conduct Handbook* published by that Society at Calgary in 1968, as amended.
ABA	*Code of Professional Responsibility* of the American Bar Association (Chicago), adopted with effect from January 1, 1970. The ABA is divided into Canons, Ethical Considerations (ECs) and Disciplinary Rules (DRs).
ABA-MR	*Model Rules of Professional Conduct* of the American Bar Association, adopted August 2, 1983.
Bennion	F.A.R., *Professional Ethics, The Consultation Professions and Their Code* (London: Charles Knight, 1969).
B.C.	Rulings of the Benchers of the Law Society of British Columbia contained in the *Professional Conduct Handbook* published by that Society at Vancouver in 1970, as amended.
CBA	*Canons of Legal Ethics* of the Canadian Bar Association adopted in 1920.
CBA-COD	*Code of Professional Conduct* of the Canadian Bar Association adopted in 1974.
IBA	*Professional Ethics,* by Sir Thomas Lund, being Book II of the International Bar Association published in 1970 by that Association (London: Sweet & Maxwell). IBA includes as an Appendix the "International Code of Ethics" of the International Bar Association adopted in 1956, as amended.
N.B.	Rules of the Barristers' Society of New Brunswick contained in the *Professional Conduct Handbook* published by that Society at Fredericton in 1971, as amended.
Ont.	Rules of Professional Conduct of the Law Society of Upper Canada contained in the *Professional Conduct Handbook* published by that Society at Toronto in 1987, as amended.
Orkin	M.M., *Legal Ethics: A Study of Professional Conduct* (Toronto: Cartwright & Jane, 1957).
Que.	*Code of Advocates,* An Act respecting the Barreau du Québec, R.S.Q. c. B-1, s. 15.
Sask.	*Canons of Legal Ethics and Etiquette* of the Law Society of Saskatchewan, published by the Benchers of that Society at Regina in 1962, as amended.

BIBLIOGRAPHY

The following is a selected bibliography of texts and other sources helpful to those concerned with matters within the general ambit of this Code:

Arthurs, H.W. and Bucknall, B.D.: *Bibliographies on the Legal Profession & Legal Education in Canada*. (1968, York University, Toronto).

Bennion, F.A.R., *supra*. For further bibliographies see at p. 238-40.

Boulton, W.W.: *Conduct and Etiquette at the Bar*. (1971 (5th ed.), Butterworths, London).

Cordery on Solicitors (6th ed. 1968; 7th ed. 1981, Butterworths, London).

Drinker, H.: *Legal Ethics*. (1965) Columbia U.P., New York).

Johnston, Q., and Hopson, D.: *Lawyers and Their Work* (1967, Bobbs-Merrill, Indianapolis).

Lund, Sir T.: *A Guide to the Professional Conduct and Etiquette of Solicitors*. (1960, The Law Society, London).

Maru, O., and Clough, R.L.: *Digest of Bar Association Ethics Opinions*. (1970, American Bar Foundation, Chicago).

Mathews, R.E.: *Problems Illustrative of the Responsibilities of Members of the Legal Profession* (2nd ed., Council on Legal Education for Professional Responsibility, New York). For further bibliographies see at pp. xii-xiv.

Orkin, M.M., *supra*. For further bibliographies see at pp. 295-96.

Pirsig, M.: *Professional Responsibility* (1970, West, St. Paul, Minn.).

Trumball, W.M.: *Materials on the Lawyer's Professional Responsibility*. (1957, Little, Brown, Boston).

INDEX

Abandoning: *see* Withdrawal
Abbreviations, 85
Abuse
  of criminal law for civil ends (III-9), 10
  of counsel, tribunals (IX-14), 39
  of process (IX-2(a)), 35
  of witnesses (IX-2(k)), 36
Accessibility: *see* Legal services
Accounting for monies, property (VIII-R, VIII-1), 31
Accounts
  interest on (XI-4), 50
  see also Fees
Administrative proceedings: *see* Tribunals
Admissions by accused: *see* Confessions
Adversary proceedings
  role for advocates in (IX-15), 39
Advertising (XIV-1, XIV-2), 63-64
Advising clients (III-R), 7-12
  candid and honest advice (III-R, III-1), 9
  criminal prosecution, impropriety of use for civil advantage (III-9), 10
  errors and omissions (III-11), 10-11
  independent advice (III-12), 11
  indicating basis of advice (III-3), 9
  non-legal matters (III-10), 10
  overconfident assurances (III-4), 9
  scope of advice (III-1, III-2, III-3, III-4), 9
  second opinion (III-5), 9
Advocate: *see* Lawyer as advocate
Affidavits (IX-5), 36
Arbitration
  between clients (V-7), 18
Associates
  as witnesses (IX-5), 36-37
  conflict of interest and (VI-3, X-2), 24, 45
  of public office holders (X-2, X-5), 45, 46
Availability: *see* Legal services
Bail (XIX-9), 82-83
Business interests
  with clients (VI-R, VI-2, VI-5, VI-6), 23-24
  with judiciary (IX-2(c)), 35
Clients
  advice to: *see* Advising clients
  arbitration between (V-7), 18

business transactions with (VI-R, VI-2, VI-5, VI-6), 23-24
debtor-creditor relationships with (VI-4), 24
definition (V-9), xi, 19
dishonesty or fraud by (III-7), 10
duty of secrecy toward (IV-4), 13
joint ventures with (VI-5), 24
public statements concerning (XVIII-2, XVIII-3), 77
right to terminate relationship with lawyer (XII-1), 53
Clients' property (VIII-R), 31-33
confidentiality (VIII-5), 31-32
definition (VIII-1), 31
delivery in the event of withdrawal (XII-8), 54
identification of (VIII-3), 31
notification of receipt (VIII-2), 31
privilege (VIII-6), 32
record-keeping (VIII-4), 31
Competence (II-R(a), II-1, II-4), 5-8
consequences of incompetence (II-9, II-10), 7
knowledge and skill (II-1, II-2, II-3, II-4, II-5), 5-6
outside interests impairing (VII-R, VII-3), 27
seeking assistance (II-6), 6
withdrawal where lacking (XII-4), 53-54
Compromise: *see* Settlement
Confessions (IX-11), 38
Confidential information (IV-R), 13-16
discussion of clients' affairs (IV-8), 8
duty of secrecy toward clients (IV-4), 13
ethical rule (IV-2, IV-5), 13, 14
in public office (X-7), 46
multiple clients (IV-6), 14
need for full and unreserved communication (IV-1), 13
prohibitions on use of (IV-5, IV-6, IV-7, IV-8), 14
re clients' property (VIII-5), 31-32
treatment in the event of withdrawal (XII-9), 55
see also Disclosures
Conflicts of interest
between clients (V-R), 17-21
between lawyer and client (VI-R, VII-4, VII-6), 23-25, 27-28
burden of proof in disciplinary proceedings (V-13), 19-20
definition (V-1, V-3), 17
disclosure of (V-4, V-5, V-6, V-13, X-4), 17-18, 19-20, 46
multiple clients and (V-10, V-11, V-12), 19
re former clients (V-8, V-9), 19
re outside interests (VII-2), 27
re public office (X-2, X-3, X-4), 45-46
withdrawal and (XII-4), 53-54

Contempt of court (IX-14), 39
Courtesy (IX-R, IX-14), 35, 39
  in public appearances (XVIII-4), 77
Criminal prosecution (III-9), 10
Cross-examination
  of other lawyers (IX-5), 36-37
Defence (IX-1, IX-10, IX-11), 35, 37-38
Disciplinary action
  for lack of integrity (I-3), 1
  re public office (X-8), 46
Disclosures
  authorized by client (IV-9), 14
  in financial matters between lawyer and client (XI-7), 50
  of agreements guaranteeing recovery (IX-17), 39
  of conflicting interests (V-4, V-5, V-6, V-13, X-4), 17-18, 19-20, 46
  of misappropriated funds (XV-1), 67
  of retainer (IV-3), 13
  required by law (IV-13, IV-14), 15
  to prevent crime (IV-11, IV-12), 15
  where laywer's conduct is in issue (IV-10), 14
  see also Confidential information
Drug use (II-7(m)), 7
Employees
  preventing breaches of confidentiality by (IV-9), 14
  supervision of (XVII-3), 73-74
Errors and omissions
  disclosure and remedy (III-11, IX-3), 10-11, 36
  insurance (III-11), 10-11
Fees (XI-R), 49-52
  apportionment and division of (XI-5), 50
  avoidance of controversy (XI-3), 50
  factors to be considered (XI-1, XI-2), 49-50
  hidden (XI-7), 50
  interest on overdue accounts (XI-4), 50
  liens for unpaid (XII-11), 55
  reduction or waiving of (XI-2), 49-50
  withdrawal for non-payment of (XII--6), 54
Fiduciary duties
  confidential information and (IV-5), 14
  re financial matters with clients (XI-7), 50
Financial obligations (XIX-7), 82
Former clients
  actions against (V-8, V-9), 19
Guilty pleas
  agreement on (IX-12), 38

Impartiality: *see* Conflicts of interest
Independent advice (III-12), 11
Integrity (I-R and generally), 1-3
    disciplinary action (I-3), 1
    fundamental quality (I-1), 1
    guiding principles (I-1, I-2), 1
    key element for each rule (I-2), 1
Insurance
    in the case of errors and omissions (III-11), 10-11
Interpretation, xi
Intoxicant use (II-7(m)), 7
Judges
    in practice after retirement or resignation (XIX-4, XIX-5), 81-82
Justice, administration of (XIII-R), 59-61
    criticism of the tribunal (XIII-4), 60
    guiding principles (XIII-1, XIII-2), 59
    improvement of (XIII-5), 60
    scope of the rule (XIII-3), 59-60
Law firms
    dissolution of (XII-13), 55
Lawyer as advocate (IX-R), 35-43
    agreement on guilty plea (IX-12), 12
    agreements guaranteeing recovery (IX-17), 39
    courtesy (IX-14), 39
    duties
        as defence counsel (IX-10, IX-11), 37-38
        as prosecutor (IX-9), 37
    duty to withdraw (IX-4), 36
    encouraging settlements (IX-8), 37
    errors and omissions (IX-3), 36
    prohibited conduct (IX-2), 35-36
    role in adversary proceedings (IX-15), 39
    scope of rule (IX-18), 39
    undertakings (IX-13), 38-39
    unmeritorious proceedings (IX-7), 37
    see also Witnesses
Legal assistants (XVII-4, XVII-5, XVII-6), 74
Legal services (XIV-R), 63-65
    accessibility and availability (XIV-1, XIV-4, XIV-5), 63, 64
    advertising (XIV-1, XIV-2, XIV-3), 63-64
    assistance in finding a lawyer (XIV-4, XIV-5, XIV-6), 64
    enforcement of restrictive rules (XIV-7), 64
    guiding principles (XIV-1, XIV-2, XIV-3), 63-64
    legal aid (XIV-5), 64
    referral services (XIV-5), 64

right to decline employment (XIV-6), 64
Letters
  response to (XVI-6), 70
  tone of (XV-3), 67
Media contacts (XVIII-6, XVIII-7, XVIII-8, XVIII-9, XVIII-10, XVIII-11, XVIII-12, XVIII-13), 78-79
Mistakes: *see* Errors and omissions
Multiple clients
  apportionment of fees (XI-5), 50
  confidential information re (IV-6), 14
  treatment in the event of withdrawal (XII-10), 55
Non-legal matters
  advice on (III-10), 10
Non-professional activities, 1
Official duties: *see* Public office
Organizations
  representation of (V-12), 19
Outside interests (VII-R), 27-29
  definition (VII-1), 27
  monies received (VII-5), 28
Partners: *see* Associates
Privilege (IV-2), 13
  with respect to clients' property (VIII-6), 32
  see also Confidential information
Professional activities
  participation in (XV-4), 67-68
Promptness (II-8), 7
Property: *see* Clients' property
Prosecutors (IX-9), 37
Public appearances (XVIII-R), 77-79
  guiding principles (XVIII-1), 77
  media contacts (XVIII-6, XVIII-7, XVIII-8, XVIII-9, XVIII-10, XVIII-11, XVIII-12, XVIII-13), 78-79
  standard of conduct in (XVIII-4, XVIII-5), 77-78
  statements concerning clients (XVIII-2, XVIII-3), 77
Public office (X-R) 45-47
  appearances before official bodies (X-5), 46
  conflicts of interest in (X-2, X-3, X-4), 45-46
  disciplinary action (X-8), 46
  disclosure of confidential information (X-7), 46
Public statements: *see* Public appearances
Quality of service (II-R(b), II-7), 6-7
  promptness (II-8), 7
  see also Competence
Questionable conduct, avoidance of (XIX-R), 81-84

    dealings with unrepresented persons (XIX-8), 82
    duties after leaving public employment (XIX-3), 81
    duty to meet financial obligations (XIX-7), 82
    guiding principles (XIX-1, XIX-2), 81
    insertion of retainer in client's will (XIX-6), 82
    retired judges (XIX-4, XIX-5), 81-82
    standard (XIX-10), 83
Recorded conversations (XV-5), 70
Responsibilities
    toward the profession (XV-R), 67-68
    toward other lawyers individually (XVI-R), 69-72
        actions against (XVI-9, XVI-10, XVI-11), 70
Retainer
    disclosure of (IV-3), 13
    insertion in client's will (XIX-6), 82
Secrecy: *see* Confidential information
Second opinions (III-5), 9
Settlement
    duty to encourage (III-6, IX-8), 10, 37
Sharp practice: *see* Technicalities
Solicitation: *see* Legal services
Special interest groups (XVIII-10), 78
Tape recording: *see* Recorded conversations
Technicalities
    reliance on (IX-10, XVI-4), 37-38, 69-70
Test cases (III-8), 10
Tribunals
    criticism of (XIII-4), 60
Unauthorized practice (XVII-R), 73-75
    employment of suspended or disbarred persons (XVII-2), 73
    guiding principles (XVII-1), 73
    restrictions on legal assistants (XVII-4, XVII-5, XVII-6), 74
    supervision of employees (XVII-3), 73-74
Undertakings (IX-13, XVI-7, XVI-8), 38-39, 70
Unrepresented persons (XIX-8), 82
Wills
    insertion of retainer in (XIX-6), 82
Withdrawal (IX-4, XII-R), 36, 53-57
    duties following (XII-8, XII-9, XII-10), 54-55
    duty of successor lawyer (XII-12), 55
    for non-payment of fees (XII-6), 54
    guiding principles (XII-1, XII-2, XII-3), 53
    liens for unpaid fees (XII-11), 55
    notice to client (XII-7), 54
    obligatory (XII-4), 53-54

optional (XII-5), 54
upon dissolution of law firm (XII-13), 55
Witnesses
communications with (IX-16), 39
prohibited conduct re (IX-2), 35-36
interviews of (IX-6), 37
lawyers as (IX-5), 36-37